**Στο γιο μου Μαξ, για το δέντρο του ~ J. E.**

**Για τον Χάμφρεϊ ~ V. C.**

*Θα κατεβάσω το φεγγάρι!*
Τίτλος πρωτοτύπου: *Bringing Down the moon*

Μετάφραση: Άννα Παπασταύρου
Διόρθωση: Άρτεμις Θεοδωρίδου


Printed in China (2009)

ΕΚΔΟΣΕΙΣ ΑΙΣΩΠΟΣ
Ματθαίου Λιούγκα 30, 166 75 Αθήνα
Τηλ.: 210 9648 215, e-mail: bagiasa@otenet.gr

ISBN 960-8240-03-4

Jonathan Emmett

# Θα Κατεβάσω το Φεγγάρι!

*Εικονογράφηση*
Vanessa Cabban

ΑΙΣΩΠΟΣ

«Θεούλη μου! Τι είναι τούτο;» φώναξε ο Μηνάς ο τυφλοπόντικας, καθώς ξεμύτισε από το χώμα μια νύχτα.

Το φεγγάρι κρεμόταν στον ουρανό πάνω από το κεφάλι του, σαν λαμπερό ασημένιο νόμισμα. Ο Μηνάς σκέφτηκε πως ήταν το πιο όμορφο πράγμα που είχε δει ποτέ.

«Ό,τι κι αν είναι,
πρέπει να το
αποκτήσω», είπε
μέσα του ο Μηνάς.
«Ξέρω τι θα κάνω.
Θα πηδήξω και
θα το κατεβάσω».

ΜΠΑΠΑ-
ΜΠΟΥΠ!

Ο Μηνάς είχε
τόσο ξεχαστεί
να προσπαθεί,
που δε σκέφτηκε
πόσο θόρυβο
έκανε, κι έτσι
ξύπνησε το λαγό
στο λαγούμι του.

«Ε, τυφλοπόντικα Μηνά!» φώναξε ο λαγός. «Τι στην ευχή κάνεις εκεί;»

«Γεια σου, λαγέ», είπε ο Μηνάς. «Προσπαθώ να κατεβάσω κείνο κει το λαμπερό πράγμα».

«Το φεγγάρι θες να πεις;» ρώτησε ο λαγός. «Ώστε έτσι το λένε, λοιπόν», είπε ο Μηνάς.

«Δε θα τα καταφέρεις ποτέ», είπε ο λαγός. «Δεν είναι τόσο κοντά όσο φαίνεται».

Όμως ο Μηνάς
δεν το έβαζε κάτω.
«Ξέρω», σκέφτηκε.
«Θα πάρω μια βέργα
και θα το κατεβάσω».
Βρήκε, λοιπόν,
μια μακριά βέργα
κι άρχισε να την
κουνάει πέρα δώθε
στο φεγγάρι.

Τόσο είχε ξεχαστεί ο Μηνάς να προσπαθεί, που σκόνταψε πάνω στον κοιμισμένο σκαντζόχοιρο.

«Μηνά!» γρύλισε ο σκαντζόχοιρος.
«Τι στην ευχή κάνεις εκεί;»

«Γεια σου, σκαντζόχοιρε», είπε ο Μηνάς.
«Προσπαθώ να κατεβάσω το φεγγάρι».

«Ποτέ δε θα τα καταφέρεις», είπε ο σκαντζόχοιρος.
«Δεν είναι τόσο κοντά όσο φαίνεται».

Όμως ο Μηνάς δεν το έβαζε κάτω. «Ξέρω», σκέφτηκε. «Θα του πετάξω κάτι και θα το κατεβάσω». Βρήκε λοιπόν μερικά βελανίδια και άρχισε να τα πετάει στο φεγγάρι.

TINK-TONK!

TINKI-TOONNK!

«Άουτς!»
έσκουξε ο σκίουρος.
«Τρελάθηκες, τυφλοπόντικα Μηνά;»

«Γεια σου, σκίουρε», είπε ο Μηνάς.
«Προσπαθώ να κατεβάσω το φεγγάρι».

«Ποτέ δε θα τα καταφέρεις», είπε ο σκίουρος.
«Δεν είναι τόσο κοντά όσο φαίνεται».

Όμως ο Μηνάς το ήθελε τόσο πολύ
το φεγγάρι, που δεν το έβαλε κάτω.
«Ξέρω», σκέφτηκε. «Θα σκαρφαλώσω
σ' ένα δέντρο και θα το πιάσω!»

Ο Μηνάς δεν είχε σκαρφαλώσει
ποτέ σε δέντρο. Ήταν δύσκολη
δουλειά και φοβόταν
να βλέπει τη γη από τόσο ψηλά!
Όμως συνέχισε ν' ανεβαίνει,
ώσπου είδε το φεγγάρι
ξαπλωμένο στις
φυλλωσιές πάνω
από το κεφάλι του.

Ο Μηνάς τεντώθηκε όσο πιο ψηλά μπορούσε. Όμως, πάνω που νόμιζε πως είχε φτάσει το φεγγάρι... γλίστρησε...

«Οχ! Άουτς! Αχ! Οοχ!!!»

...και με μια τελευταία τούμπα βρέθηκε

**ΠΛΑΤΣ!**

μέσα σε μια νερολακκούβα.

«Παμπόνηρο φεγγάρι!» σκέφτηκε ο Μηνάς. «Λίγο ακόμα και θα σε είχα στα χέρια μου!» Τότε πρόσεξε κάτι να κολυμπάει μέσα στη νερολακκούβα. Ήταν χλομό και ζαρωμένο, όμως ο Μηνάς το αναγνώρισε αμέσως.

«Το φεγγάρι», ψιθύρισε ο Μηνάς.
«Φαίνεται πως κατρακυλήσαμε μαζί».
Άπλωσε την πατούσα του να πιάσει
το φεγγάρι. Όμως μόλις το άγγιξε,
αυτό έγινε κομμάτια
και χάθηκε.

Ο Μηνάς κάθισε στη νερολακκούβα κι έκλαιγε. Ο λαγός, ο σκαντζόχοιρος κι ο σκίουρος ήρθαν τρέχοντας κοντά του.

«Είσαι καλά, τυφλοπόντικα Μηνά;» ρώτησε ο λαγός.

«Εγώ καλά είμαι!» κλαψούρισε ο Μηνάς.
«Το φεγγάρι, όμως, δεν είναι!
Το έριξα κάτω και το έσπασα...
κι ήταν ΤΟΣΟ όμορφο... και... και...
τώρα πια δε θα το δω ποτέ ξανά!»

«Αχ, Μηνά», είπε ο λαγός,
«δεν μπορεί να έριξες κάτω το φεγγάρι».

«Και δε γίνεται να το έσπασες»,
είπε ο σκαντζόχοιρος.

«Και σίγουρα θα το ξαναδείς»,
είπε ο σκίουρος. «Κοίτα!»

Ψηλά στον ουρανό, το φεγγάρι
πρόβαλλε αργά, πίσω από ένα σύννεφο.

«Ο!» ψιθύρισε ο Μηνάς,
«κι είναι όμορφο όπως πρώτα!»

Τυφλοπόντικας και λαγός,
σκαντζόχοιρος και σκίουρος,
στάθηκαν και θαύμαζαν το φεγγάρι.

«Είναι όμορφο», είπε ο λαγός.

«Πολύ όμορφο!» είπε ο σκαντζόχοιρος.

«Πανέμορφο, στ' αλήθεια!»
είπε ο σκίουρος.

«Πράγματι»,
είπε ο Μηνάς.
«Όμως ΔΕΝ είναι
τόσο κοντά
όσο φαίνεται!»

Many happy returns of the day Ruth,

Much love,

Richard + Sue

28.5.08

CHARLIE WAITE

# LANDSCAPE

THE STORY OF 50 FAVOURITE PHOTOGRAPHS

COLLINS & BROWN

Distributed in the United States and Canada by
Sterling Publishing Co, 387 Park Avenue South, New York, NY 10016, USA.



British Library Cataloguing-in-Publication Data:
A CIP catalogue record for this book is available from
the British Library.

10 9 8 7 6 5 4 3 2

ISBN 10: 1 84340 189 4
ISBN 13: 9 78184 3401 896

Commissioning Editor: Chris Stone
Project Editor: Carly Madden
Designer: Simon Daley
Proofread by Sharon Amos

Reproduction by Classicscan, Singapore
Printed by SNP Leefung, China

This book can be ordered direct from the publisher.
Contact the marketing department, but try your bookshop first.

www.anovabooks.com

# CONTENTS

# INTRODUCTION

I can remember with absolute clarity the moment I first became captivated by photography. When I was about 11, my father, a skilled and ardent photographer, turned my bedroom into a makeshift darkroom. After setting up the equipment, we were ready to start printing from a roll of film, and he reached for the lightswitch. In a bewitching fraction of a second, he had exchanged the white light of my room, for the curious soft red glow of the safelights – and in that instant I was spellbound. With great excitement and anticipation, I waited for what was to follow...

A year before I was born, my father was stationed in Berlin where he was devising, with the aid of a slide rule, the astonishing logistics of what would become one of the great humanitarian aid accomplishments: the Berlin Airlift. In what little spare time he had, he relaxed by making portrait photographs of my two elder sisters. Some twelve years later, with our faces bathed in shadowless red, he showed me magic. In half an inch of amber liquid and with the gentle rocking motion of a rectangular white enamelled dish, those images of my sisters reappeared to their open-mouthed young brother.

In less than an hour I was rushing around our house, looking for anyone I could find to show the ten by eight inch print of Romilly and Joanna which my father and I had made. Perhaps that frantic race into every room, desperate to find someone to whom I could show the magic that we had conjured up together, embodies in some way the moment in which I realised that I would always be enthralled by making images. Despite now knowing something of the chemistry, physics and science of the photographic process, I never feel separated from that first moment when, as an impressionable eleven-year-old boy, I saw emerging in a dish of developer an image on a piece of paper.

At 17 and with one single qualification to my name, I left school and joined a repertory theatre in the hope that after some two years as an assistant stage manager, I would become an actor. My ambition was realized, though not fully; I achieved my Equity card (still kept up to date) and became an actor. Work was of course spasmodic: a summer season on the end of a pier at an English seaside resort, minor roles in repertory theatre productions, a few small television appearances, one third-rate movie and an exciting year in a theatre in Nairobi, Kenya, playing anything from a small child in *Anne of Green Gables* to a sinister coin-spinning gangster in an Edgar Wallace thriller.

I had borrowed my father's beautifully engineered Voigtlander camera for the year that I lived and worked in Africa, and used it only once or twice. In an entire year, in one of the most wonderfully photographic countries in the world, I took perhaps thirty-six photographs.

Towards the end of the seventies, and acknowledging the precarious nature of the theatre, I chose to abandon a profession where I seemed to have little control over my destiny. Instead I took a one-year intensive course in photographic theory, from which I emerged in 1978. Then when anyone asked what I did, I answered, with some hesitation, that I was a portrait photographer for actors.

I enjoyed meeting actors, for I had left the profession reluctantly, or, as many an actor has said, 'It left me'. So for many years, I took photographs of actors for a living and of landscapes (albeit seemingly without purpose), for myself. One Saturday in winter, I was asked by a publisher whom I had met by chance, whether I also took landscape photographs. I replied somewhat boldly that I was in fact a landscape photographer. The performance must have been convincing as he asked for my telephone number, mentioning that he would like to see my portfolio.

Within a week of meeting the publisher, I had a commission for my first book. The book took nearly a year to complete and I came to realize, during that intensive year of photography and after many hours of waiting for everything to 'come right', that my photography would no longer be about merely taking photographs. It would be about adopting an approach which was essentially far removed from acquisitiveness, and much closer to the idea of 'reception'.

That first year of full-time photography represented a turning point. The more I engaged with what I was photographing, and the more immersed in it I became, the greater the reward I experienced.

No longer was the camera a device to record, as I had once regarded it. In those early and difficult years of my photography I learned that the camera could be an instrument for artistry. I encountered pockets of photographers all of whom had realized long before me, that photography was a wonderfully creative medium. I spent hours in bookshops, seeking anything I could find on photography, on any photography; I had a voracious appetite. Secondhand booksellers who may have been uncertain as to whether their books on photography would find a buyer, were left smiling at the till as I plucked them from the musty shelves. Time and again, I picked the books of photographs by Ansel Adams; to my mind he had the qualities of a fine artist, but was also a meticulous technician, and these combined to demonstrate the pure craft of photography of the very highest excellence. Here was a style of photography that expressed some deeper meaning to me.

As my photography developed, so did a greater understanding of the sacred nature of the earth. My responses to my surroundings grew to become ones of reverence, wonder and joy. The camera was the vehicle for the transmission of these sentiments, and the resulting image was the manifestation of that relationship.

As I continue, I find that paradoxically I need to impose a degree of order onto what I am photographing: I can not tolerate 'a looseness'. I find that much of my photography involves construction, of waiting for elements to happily interlock and align themselves; it is about a process of achieving a cohesion of balance and, to a degree, of design. Often the image has in fact already been made without a camera. It can vividly infuse itself into my consciousness without aberration, without fault, perfect in every way. It becomes a question of pre-natal recognition rather than post-natal acknowledgment.

Then, against this backdrop of the pursuit of perfection, a struggle of sorts begins: the attempt to reconcile the image that I see in the ground-glass screen with the uncontaminated image that resides, at first, in my imagination. This is where reward can often be found. But then the most agonizing of dilemmas can take place, with that most wretched of words worming its way into any artistic endeavour: compromise. When we already know what could be possible, how much harder it is to give way to compromise, for lack of those elements that we so desire should imbue the image.

Of course, more often than not, light is the great catalyst that can reveal and finally yield the image one yearns for. The compromises to which I have succumbed with past images I have made, continue to haunt me. The fifty images appearing in this book represent photography where the minimum of compromises had to be reached.

As my photography developed, so did a greater understanding of the sacred nature of the earth. My responses to my surroundings grew to become ones of reverence, wonder and joy. The camera was the vehicle for the transmission of these sentiments, and the resulting image was the manifestation of that relationship

I am often challenged by the following question from those who do not care to take photographs. Does the camera intrude upon what would otherwise be a straightforward human response to an object of wonder? Does the camera get in the way? I do not believe so. On the contrary, to photograph the sky reflecting and re-expressing itself in opalescence upon the surface of a lake at dawn, to photograph ten thousand dancing leaves of a silver birch flickering their brilliance in an October light, to raise the lens toward a brooding sky that has the pathos of a Wagnerian symphony, surely draws the landscape photographer into the very heart of each experience. Landscape photography offers a wonderful amplification and intensification of all that is visual. The landscape photographer has a visual agility that is acute. My motto tends to be: 'Antennae up and in reception mode'.

I am often asked which of my images I am most attached to. It is a question that I am unable to answer, for tomorrow it may be different. Perhaps though, when in pursuit of the many daily demands of human existence, we might all contemplate the definitive landscape image: the photograph from space of planet Earth.

# 50 FAVOURITE PHOTOGRAPHS

# The Jura
## France

Film **Kodak Ektachrome 64**
Camera **Hasselblad 6cmx 6cm**
Lens **50mm**
Exposure **½ sec f.22**
Filters **ND 1 stop graduated and 81B**

Of all the images that epitomize my love of landscape photography, it is this one of a wooded valley in the Jura.

The Jura is tucked in between Alsace and Savoie and like many regions of France is still relatively unexplored. I had stayed the night in St Claude, north west of Geneva, and I remember well the pounding rain on the roof of my lodgings. As in Tuscany, rain in the night can fill me with expectation and the promise of fine light but I had no idea when I woke that morning, what I would find in the sky.

I had woken before dawn, the rain had stopped and with a certain amount of optimism I chose to climb up to get some elevation. In the autumn, the sun rises almost due east and to be photographing on an east-west axis in the early hours of daylight often gives one the best chance. I turned the corner (it is almost always about turning corners) and behold, there was one of the loveliest landscapes I had ever seen in my life.

The foreground was a blaze of light and yet the most remarkable thing was the lack of direct sunlight shining on the scene. The landscape was lit with a relatively flat light, but it seemed to come from within the trees, not from light falling upon them. The whole place radiated golden warmth back to me and the camera.

The colour of the sky was equally warm but I added an 81B mild amber filter and a neutral density graduated to hold the subtle and very pleasing nuances in the sky – the 81B was to ensure that any grey in the sky took on a little additional warmth. Nuances in the sky are precious and must be preserved. A fine sky is to be relished as often as possible.

The hanging mist in the distant valley, contained conveniently by the sloping hills either side, is lent a backdrop by the distant hill. I had not realized what a crucial role the back hill plays in this photograph. Had it not been there, the mist may have not been legible and the distance would have just petered out and simply merged into the sky.

I often show this image in talks. It is always the last to be projected onto the screen – still, in my view, the very best way to enjoy a photograph. I still gasp when I see it, often eight feet square. There was complete union between me and the landscape that morning. I felt for a moment that all was understood, no questions needed to be asked about anything. For a moment I thought that only I had been privy to this wonderful revelation. Perhaps when it is at its best, this, for me, is what lies at the core of landscape photography: the extraordinarily intimate and intense contact between me and all that loveliness.

At the end of it all I was strangely exhausted, yet I had not moved a metre.

Film **Fuji Velvia**
Camera **Hasselblad 6cmx6cm**
Lens **150mm**
Exposure **1/4 f. 32**
Filters **Polarizer**

# Willoughby Hedge, Wiltshire
## England

This dear tree is one of my best friends in the West Country. I have known it (although 'it' is too poor an address for such a chum) for more than twenty-five years. I have seen this fellow through every stage of the seasons, in so much leaf as to surely weigh an extra ton, and dressed in shimmering bronze with the side light of an October afternoon. I have stopped and greeted my tree in fog, driving rain, sleet and snow, in the fiercest of gales and in the stillest air, during the furnace heat of high summer. We are pals, this tree and I.

With all this being so, how could I not place the dearest of trees right into the middle of the frame? Anything else would have been unthinkable. I remember looking through the 6cm x 6cm ground-glass screen and realizing that this could not be a square image; it was clear to me that to have dropped the tree into a square of blue which was so intense and widespread, would have resulted in the tree being overwhelmed and literally sunk in a sea of blue.

There are interchangeable backs with my camera that allow for a 6cm x 6cm format to be exchanged for 6cm x 6.45cm one. When I feel I am warming to an image, like the hide and seek games we played as children, there is a wonderful feeling of brand new discovery, and as I looked anew at the scene now framed by a rectangle, it began to work.

There were patches of green amongst the blue flax and I became distressed about this. The blue is broken up by strips of green on the back hill; the diagonal banding gives a sense of depth by breaking the continuity of blue in the foreground. Then the horizontal line where this seam takes place seemed unsatisfactory. I was wondering whether to wait and come back in a day or so in the hope that the flax might have flourished enough to outweigh the patches of green. A modicum of sun arrived and brushed the top of the tree. In a moment these considerations left me, and I made an exposure.

I look at this photograph and am always thankful for that splash of light: it delivered the slightest shadow below the tree, while, thankfully, the very lowest branches did not appear to have merged with it. Had they done so, the tree would not have identified itself sufficiently and this is most especially true of this shortest of tree trunks. Another five thousand leaves on the near branch and the stub of the trunk would have been concealed.

# Sossusvlei
## Namibia

My first sighting of the giant-star shaped dunes of Sossusvlei in Namibia produced in me a deep audible gasp. Here was a landscape brimming over with gravitas, completely off the 'awe and wonder' scale.

I had made many journeys since to these phenomenal dunes. I had seen them from the first light of day to the last, and despite trying over a four-year period to achieve an image that would evoke their monumental grandeur, I never felt that I had mastered them.

Just before dawn one March morning, when the air had become still after a storm, I set off down to the dunes. Within half an hour, I realized that if the blue and magenta clouds continued to hang over the dunes, and if a gap in the cloud behind

Film **Fuji Velvia**
Camera **Fuji 6cmx17cm**
Lens **300mm**
Exposure **3 secs f.64**
Filters **Polarizer**
**ND 1 stop graduated**

me to the east were to allow the first red/orange rays of sunlight to pass through, I might be fortunate enough to make an image.

I motioned to the Landrover driver to speed up. If the wonderful canopy of violet sky receded too far to the west, then, despite the format of 6cm x 17cm, I may have to contend with a piece of pure blue sky appearing at the top of the frame. If there is continuity of form and mood in a sky, introducing another segment distracts the eye of the observer from where you wish it to settle.

The car hurled itself into a sudden spinning stop. In a flurry of sand and dust, I ran with the large cannon-like camera to the point where I could lay the small bobbly trees along the bottom of the frame. They were like the front of a stage, providing a dark foundation upon which the giant dunes could sit. Just after 7am the gap in the sky widened and the burning red-hot rays of that early sun slammed full-on against the already red dunes. With one thousand decibels of Wagner's Tannhäuser echoing all around me, pure joy enveloped me as I depressed the shutter.

# Chateau Sully

## France

There must be thousands of chateaux throughout France, many of which have been sympathetically restored, while others, despite their great age, look as if the builders have left just the day before.

One of my favourites is the delicate Chateau Sully on the Sologne border, which sits on the southern edge of the formidable river Loire. Sully is the last pretty chateau that the Loire sees before it pours itself through Orleans.

Chateau Sully is sometimes grouped with the great Chateaux of the Loire, but Burgundians often regard it as their own. I have stood on the eastern side of the moat on a few occasions, remembering a happy day in 1980, when the chateau was lit as if by a theatre spotlight. Visitors were scampering from the rain as I crouched over my already wet camera bag. To be in the corridor of change, lying in wait for the passing storm to be replaced by hard contrasting direct light guarantees thrilling anticipation. Even if the image fails to materialize as I would wish, the pursuit and the attempt always leaves me with sufficient satisfaction and I will return.

On the previous day, I had seen the chateau in a light which many may call a 'lovely day': in other words, clear blue monotonous sky. Indeed it was a lovely day, but not for someone who needed 'information' in the sky. During the night I had heard the wonderful sound of rain and wind driving against the dormer window of my hotel room. Things were looking up. The following morning, I left for Sully with the windscreen wipers panicking, as they seem to, when at full speed. Then began the wait (how aptly named I am), and within three hours I found myself standing upright with clearing skies behind me. I was about to find myself in the heart of my corridor. I remember praying (a common practice) that nothing should undermine my intention of producing an image that played out the great drama of a forbidding sky behind a brightly lit chateau, while the wonderful phenomenon of a perfect reflection prevailed in the foreground. My prayers were not to beg that a breeze should not manifest itself, or that the light should not change: I was confident of both these crucial factors. I was praying hard for the most simple and in some ways the most facile of prayers to be answered, and, thankfully, it was: that a duck should not choose that precise moment to descend in a skid across my immaculate mirrored water.

Film **Fuji 50asa**
Camera **Hasselblad 6cmx6cm**
Lens **50mm**
Exposure **1/8th f.22**
Filters **ND 1 stop graduated**

Chateau Sully, France

# Amiens

## France

Film **Fuji Velvia**
Camera **Hasselblad 6cmx6cm**
Lens **50mm**
Exposure **1 sec f.22**
Filters **Polarizer**

In 2002, I had thought that a one-week journey to the Somme would yield just one image and this certainly looked to be the case on the final day. I was returning home, feeling satiated and encouraged in the knowledge that the image of the poplar trees in the Somme (see page 72) would be right: that it would 'work'.

There had been much rain some weeks before, and often I find that this is a good time to travel. Setting off in good weather means one has missed the transition; better to set off in poor weather to be there for the change.

I saw these trees in a flash as I came around a corner outside Amiens, and within a few moments, I was wearing waterproof boots and hobbling around in mud, trying to get my tripod fixed in the spot where I wanted to set up. As I prepared I hoped that there would be no wind: the reflection was crucial, to say the least.

I was hoping too that the blue would stay in the sky, for it is this blue that brings the image together; I have tried to imagine these trees in poor weather, and am so grateful that we had the sun. I stood amid this water world in absolute stillness, with just the noise of the odd passing car to cut through the quiet moments. After only a few moments, I noticed the narrow belts of dampness around each tree indicating that the water level was dropping. If I were to wait perhaps a further half-hour, these dark belts would become more pronounced and help to delineate the division between trunk and water surface. I was pleased I waited, as the strap marks around each tree play an important role in understanding what is going on.

I find the reflection here very satisfying, but I am quite prepared to be alone in thinking this. After all, I was there with the atmosphere, the feeling of satisfaction after making the image of the architectural nave of poplars, the pleasure at seeing those dark belts around the base of the trees and the blue sky expanding above.

After the image had been made, I had the idea of paddling into the lagoon, if only to connect with the essence of the place; but the water quickly spilled over the top of my boots, and I knew that I had gone far enough.

# Spluga Pass
## Italy

Film **Fuji Velvia**
Camera **Hasselblad 6cmx6cm**
Lens **50mm**
Exposure **2secs f.22**
Filters **ND graduated 1 stop**

A good many years ago, I was working in Lombardy photographing the fine Lakes of Como, Maggiore, Garda and the beautiful Iseo, and after a long month away, chose to head home north through the Spluga pass. Almost on the same latitude as the still swanky St Moritz, the Spluga pass takes the traveller out of the top of Italy into the chalets, green baize pastures and cow-bells of Switzerland. The way through is hard. Though not by any means the highest of passes, the Spluga is composed of switch-back hairpins that send many a passenger reaching for the cognac. At two thousand and fifteen metres at its summit, it is arduous enough. I was travelling as I often did, with my exceptional mother. She was exceptional in many ways, but one of her great merits was her ability to read maps. She loved maps and could read them quickly in order to make snap judgements.

Passing one of the thousand bends, I saw the mountains with steamy clouds round their outline and a little sun just playing in between. The twin summits were revealed for what I thought would be only a moment, and the lower slopes hung in shadow. What a thing it would be if I could find a rock that echoed something of the mountains beyond. It is often informative for the spectator to learn something of the substance of what lies beyond, by revealing similar landscape in the foreground.

After a fair amount of kindergarten mountaineering – no more than jumping from rock to rock to find the right one – I at last discovered the perfect article. It was quite touching how fond of this rock I became. It fitted so snugly into the distant landscape that I felt that it had been made for me, and for this moment, and all that I needed was that it should light itself up. Light was vital to provide not only the contrast needed to separate it from the shadow behind, but also to reveal the modelling of the traumatized and splintered rock, its texture and its folds.

The shrouds of cloud that often hang conveniently or inconveniently over mountain peaks have, of course, explanations of warm and cold air masses. But to the landscape photographer, explanation is of no help whatsoever. It was a game of cat and mouse. The tip of the left-hand mountain taunted me with its disappearing act. When it revealed itself, what little light which had arrived on my foreground rock became diminished and slipped away; when it clothed itself in cloud again, my rock became almost incandescent with light. And so it went on; light on rock: no peak; no light on rock: peak revealed. Imagine the peak of the mountain to the left hidden from view and no light in the dips. I was not going to stand for it. And then, with one final huff, the peak emerged and light arrived to order on my foreground rock.

I remember shouting out loud, 'Hallelujah!'. My mother asked why I was so jubilant. Just managed to make my image, Mum. Just.

Film **Kodak recording film**
Camera **Nikon 35mm**
Lens **28mm**
Exposure **Not recorded**

# St Enodoc, Cornwall
## England

From a very early age, my mother and father took me and my two elder sisters Joanna and Romilly to North Cornwall for sailing holidays. We did what all children have done when holidaying in Cornwall; taunted the sea with our loudest screams, sat on the pasties, swam with the dog, made the dog shake over the parents, tripped over guy ropes, brought sand into the house, got fed and slept deeply.

Many years later, I was sure my parents would like another dog, and without consulting them, I got a rescue dog for them. Joseph entered the family.

In Cornwall again, I took Joseph along the Northern shore of the Camel estuary and after passing the magical St Enodoc church, once buried under the sand, I turned towards the water and the dunes. I had happy memories of hysterical stumblings down these steep slopes, spinning and somersaulting to the bottom, with Saxon, our first dog, following in a rather more dignified fashion on four legs.

With these memories in my mind, I sat on the lower slope of a dune, gazing across towards Padstow and the fluttering bar, with the tide speeding backwards from Wadebridge. Looking up, I saw Joseph sitting quite still and contentedly looking at the same gentle scene as me. Neither of us were particularly focused, just happy to look across one of the loveliest estuaries in Britain. We were both in a contemplative mood. Just to the left of him was a dead claw-like stump of a tree. The sand in the foreground was a mess of stones, small twigs and footprints.

I had with me a 35mm camera, one lens and one roll of a little-used film: Kodak recording film, which has more application in the world of surveillance than in lumpy Cornish dunes. The characteristic of this film is high sensitivity to light, and accordingly the grain of the silver halide crystals is apparent. The effect results in the entire image appearing to be covered in a wash of grit.

The sky was unremarkable: no cloud, no identity. Unlike almost every other occasion when an image has been made, where so much has been pondered on and weighed up, there was no small voice beckoning me to devote time and energy to making an image here, and yet I did, though almost half-heartedly.

To the right was Joseph with haunches prominent, and to the left, the lifeless tree; not much to hang an image on but there was an enigmatic feel to this unusual scene which I felt, through my photography, I might try and make clear to myself.

Looking at this image of Joseph and the tree stimulates me to ask questions and, with minimal reference points, challenges my imagination for explanation. It is an image of a dead tree and a roguish dog Joseph, both planted on a coarse landscape. To Joseph I guess it was simply about enjoying the view.

# Pennsylvania
## USA

Film **Kodak T400CN**
Camera **Ricoh GR21**
Lens **28mm**
Exposure **Not recorded**

A year or so ago, I was invited to Pennsylvania to visit Amish country. I had no idea what to expect and, while I had seen the film *Witness* a few years earlier, I was unfamiliar with these people and their unorthodox way of life.

While I have photographed many people with their permission, I am always reluctant to photograph people without it – it seems invasive and intimidating.

On this occasion, I had set up my tripod, for, not one hundred yards away, in the morning dankness, I saw six muscular shire horses pulling a plough, with the Amish farmer driving the team from behind. Steam rose from the animals' backs, and the driver bellowed out instructions. This was a scene from another era. Then he saw me. He snarled and shouted across the rutted field: 'Don't you have anything better to do than photograph me?' In an instant, I felt like throwing my camera away. I had brutally intruded upon this man's way of life with the wretched thing. I felt appropriately contrite and slunk away.

Despite this, there was a second time when I was guilty of intrusion but I hoped that I was being more discreet. I was further away, and a group of Amish people was walking towards a barn to participate in a Sunday gathering. The light was poor, but for once – I never thought I would say this – light had no relevance. All I cared was that there was enough for simple illumination.

The way in which the buggies had been seemingly marooned was perfect. I remember praying that the owners would leave at least two of them to be set off against the white barn. The carriage far left, with its lopsided tilt, was perfect, and when the owners walked away, leaving this wonderful composition, I could have hugged them. The design was there and now a story needed to unfold.

Then it was the turn of the congregation. I hoped they would remain separate. If they bunched up they would create a black mass that would be distracting to the viewer and provide insufficient information. As they marched towards the building, I had perhaps 30 seconds to act, but it was long enough. From the man at the head of the line, with his right heel up indicating natural motion, back towards the two in conversation, to the stragglers – it all seemed right. Even the small black window above the first man pleased me; and that foot was crucial.

Were they aware of me? Perhaps, but they did not show it. And I enjoyed what I had learnt, making this image. All the components of triangles, rectangles and circles offset one another perfectly and set the stage for the arrival of the human form. As I watched, a micro moment of live theatre had unfolded before me, prevailed for a moment, and was gone. Thankfully a camera shutter opening and closing found its way into the heart of this moment and secured it.

Pennsylvania, USA

# Valensole, Provence
## France

Film **Fujichrome 50 ASA**
Camera **Hasselblad**
Lens **150mm**
Exposure **¼ second f.22/f.32**
Filters **Polarizer**

In the early winter of 1986 I drove up from the lively Cote d'Azur, which despite its decline over the past 40 years, still manages to conjure up imagery of glamorous living, sleek yachts and blackjack tables.

For me a better place to be was in the remote and equally rich lavender fields of the high plains of Valensole. My first sighting was not of lavender flowers but of the plants in winter looking like giant porcupines, betraying nothing of the sea of purple that they would become in the coming scalding July heat.

Years earlier I had arrived here when the lavender had been almost all harvested and the only compensation for such disappointment was to drive through the smoke from the burning waste with all windows of the car wide open to allow the fragrance of smoky lavender to enter. Not even Chanel could match it.

I had passed this building a good many times that day, dismissing it as an utterly dreary utilitarian construction without charm or interest; a lump of asbestos and cement. Returning I realized that I had missed the light at the gable end of the building that placed it into stark relief: once seen, then the rest of the building seemed to fall into place with the surroundings. The corrugated roof related albeit tenuously (due to the angle) to the diagonal lines in the lavender fields and the two trees either side set off the tableau. The removal of a UV filter provided the pronounced blue of mountain and sky and, with no cloud to interrupt the arrangement, the result is to me surprisingly pleasing. The lavender appeared a little ragged, with tufts of green here and there, but I felt disinclined to tamper with that. I did succumb to the minutest restoration of the tree to the right; this seems harmless enough.

There are times when the placement of a building or tree in the very centre of the image seems too obvious, too crass and yet this seemed exactly the thing to do – in fact, there appeared to be no choice and so with some bravado, I did so. The anchor to the image must be the extremely brightly lit gable end of the building and if you conceal this with your finger, the image disintegrates entirely. The polarizing filter was used here to both increase saturation and remove a little white light reflection, which even on a porous surface such as the cement walls had some significant effect.

I passed here a year or so ago and my shed had been demolished, along with the two innocent trees.

# Lucignano d'Asso, Tuscany

## Italy

I look at this photograph with great fondness and am always transported to another place and time. To either side of the Via Cassia, which runs from Siena to Rome, there is a network of unpaved roads, each known as a *strada bianca*.

There must be many hundreds of kilometres of these white roads and you can always tell who lives along one of them, as their cars are usually coated with a dusting of fine white powder. Farmers, who, over the centuries, became accustomed to working in this lumpy landscape, habitually used the roads. Now the wonderful network provides access to the thousands of converted farmhouses in the area.

Every year for the past twenty I have explored these tracks, and I have become fond of one in particular: the road to Lucignano d'Asso, a hamlet near Asciano.

I had seen this chapel several times a good few years ago, always in rather harsh sunlight, which created too much contrast at the end of the day. On an unusually chilly spring morning, I went there once again, and found it virtually shadowless as I had hoped. But what lies behind my love of this modest little place? The two rather tired-looking cypress trees have been planted unusually close to the chapel and the orange door was new since I was here last. I have always wondered about the third cypress, and while some may say it makes no difference to the photograph, I feel it might have been better without it. But to have tightly cropped into the chapel on the right would have cramped it, and to remove it through imaging software was not something I cared to do. So there the third cypress tree remains.

I often enjoy covering over small elements within a photograph to demonstrate the effect their removal has on the overall cohesion of the image. The circular glassless window certainly plays a part and with my thumb placed over it, an element is removed that contributes to the chapel's charm. You could argue that I might have made the photograph even if there had been no window. Perhaps so. But the round window and the hint of the ridge end between the twin cypress trees are significant to me.

Considerations of this nature should in my view preoccupy the landscape photographer all the time. The omission or inclusion of the smallest element in an image can have a considerable bearing, not only on one's own evaluation of the image to be made, but also on the response that will be drawn from the spectator.

After packing up, I tried the door of the chapel. It was locked. I would have liked to have gone in and sat for a while. Perhaps you could say that this photograph of Lucignano d'Asso holds the same special mystery for me as it might for the spectator; neither of us knows what is inside.

Film **Fuji Velvia**
Camera **Hasselblad 6cmx6cm**
Lens **80mm**
Exposure **1/8th sec f.22**

Lucignano d'Asso, Tuscany, Italy

# Sinalunga, Tuscany

## Italy

In Tuscany numerous cypress trees punctuate the landscape. For the most part they are randomly scattered about this ravishing scenery. But they are often planted as avenues to manor houses in the same way as fine limes or beech trees were used in the UK to emphasize the experience of arrival and departure. In 1995 I remember seeing one example of an elderly converted farmhouse, which, like so many, sat high on this typical landscape. Planted with great precision was the now mandatory line of young cypress trees. I returned to the same house some years later and with envy looked upon the new conversion with its fine proportions and perfectly matched stone work. The one hundred or so young cypresses still looked as diminutive as when I first saw them and, for the time being anyway, a guest's arrival would not be quite as grand as it might be in thirty years time. The cypress grows slowly.

The cypress has always had associations with death and cemeteries. Few cemeteries in southern Europe would be without a cluster of flame-like cypresses. The fragrance from their resin is never far away, and they can even be seen, deformed and tormented, in the 'art' of topiary, a technique I do not care for.

While working on a book on the region, I had passed this particular tree many times, and each occasion had cheered me, reminding me that only a few miles remained before reaching the farm I was staying in. It had occurred to me once or twice to stop, but each time I thought of it, I drove on. I had seen the tree lit with bright side lighting on many occasions and often with splendid skies, but the various combinations of good skies and light never seemed worthy of an image.

To isolate any tree imbues it with stateliness and nobility. In this soft light, the solitary young cypress took on a dignity that I had not recognized in the three weeks of our relationship. It had rained for some hours and the wind had blown through the steep streets of Sinalunga, leaving me deflated. Incessant rain can weigh heavy. On the return route, with no images made, I passed my tree, and, with uplifted spirits, I suddenly saw that now was most certainly the time to capture it.

Cypress foliage is very light absorbing. Even in full sunlight the matt green, which is often covered in a fine white dust from the *strada bianca*, reflects little light. Also, I hesitate to allow a vertical element to bisect a horizontal such as the horizon. But here the receding land cannot be used as a measure of distance: the far horizon is so imprecise that it peters out to join the sky, so the division between the girth of the cypress and the horizon is gentle and not aggressive.

The surrounding landscape east of Sinalunga is mute, with an amber warmth and little contrast; within this gentle rolling panarama stands my dark and familiar cypress tree, as if to make a point.

Film **Fuji Velvia**
Camera **Hasselblad 6cmx6cm**
Lens **50mm**
Exposure **1 sec f.22**
Filters **81B**

# Delphi
## Greece

Film **Fuji 50asa**
Camera **Hasselblad 6cmx6cm**
Lens **80mm**
Exposure **Not recorded**
Filters **Polarizer and 81a and ND 1 stop graduated**

I had got to know Delphi and something of its history and oracle over a period of a few days, and full of all this, I was eager to acquire more knowledge, and hoped I might do so in conjunction with my photography. This did not work; it never does. On the whole, landscape photography is all-consuming.

I had chosen my vantage point high above the Temple of Athena. It was a precarious ledge with just enough space for the tripod, bag, camera and me. It is always very reassuring to have worked out where the ideal spot should be for the photograph to be made and there are times when I have managed this up to a year before I have attempted a photograph.

The weather was forecast as changeable, which is certainly more useful to a landscape photographer than consistency. I was the first to arrive at Delphi that day, and the blanket of blue sky above me induced modest despair. When engaged in the pursuit of a photograph, I can think of nothing more depressing than plain blue sky. With no photography in mind, of course, it is wonderful.

I took up my position and feeling confident that the monotonous blue would ultimately be replaced by something interesting, I waited.

I can identify with those who are fascinated by meteorology and the anomalies of the weather. Landscape photographers are equally concerned as to what may take place above and I certainly spend a great deal of time looking up to see what weather system may be approaching. I have learnt one thing over the years: that trying to pre-empt what the sky will do when conditions are uncertain is impossible, but that powerlessness makes the entire process particularly enjoyable.

I have never known it to rain so hard and so suddenly, in such a short space of time. I have experienced rain in parts of Africa where it became very painful on the head, but for some irrational reason I never expected to encounter the same sheer downward force of water in Greece. But by mid-afternoon and still perched in my eyrie, I could see to the west a defined line of blue, and soon a good breeze pushed the bulk of grey cloud away to allow a splash of sun to bathe the temple in light. It all seemed fitting, and I made an exposure. Then, as the light grew more intense, the unimaginable happened. A coach arrived and more than a hundred students were soon swarming over the landscape in front of me. From my high vantage point, I pleaded to the leader to ask the students to stand just fifty metres to the left. To my astonishment, he complied: one hundred young students are, in fact, inches from the edge of this image. All done without consulting the oracle.

# Cienfuegos
## Cuba

Film **Kodak T400CN**
Camera **Hasselblad Xpan**
Lens **45mm**
Exposure **Not recorded**
Filters **25a red filter**

A few years ago, I went to Cuba with my daughter Ella. I wanted to do a reconnaissance before bringing a group of photographers here on a workshop.

Cuba has a turbulent history and it is important for a visitor to be acquainted with some of it. Cuba is not only about cigars, flamenco and the Tropicana. Once it was about the accumulation of great fortunes and about poor people, then and still, dealing valiantly with a considerable amount of hardship.

Two hundred kilometres or so south east of Havana is Cienfuegos, a town laid out like Manhattan and with some wonderful neo-classical architecture. By the turn of the 18th century, agriculture in Cuba was dominated by sugar-cane. The immense wealth that it brought allowed the sugar barons to construct the biggest status symbols possible: the palace and the Casa de la Cultura, or what remains of it, which is one of the finest buildings in Cienfuegos.

In the Casa de la Cultura, the sound of loud Spanish guitar music encouraged me to climb up to what I thought was the topmost floor. Up there, I stood outside a room made mostly of glass where there was a battered cassette player and a group of children learning to dance flamenco. So involved were they in their lesson that I passed by unnoticed. Beyond, I found a magnificent staircase and this was to give me a good two hours of pleasure. Superbly carved, it seemed to have been waiting for me. I was overjoyed with the nature of the cloud, but longed for it to move away to the left, allowing the entire balustrade to be set against the darker blue. However, it was clear that this image should be made in black and white, of that there was no question. The camera was a Hasselblad Xpan with a 45mm lens and Konica infra red film. I used a 25A red filter, which allows a proportion of the visible spectrum to pass through, rather than the opaque filter, which I do not care for. I was in need of a vertical panoramic format and the Xpan provided it. The image has been cropped.

There are times in my photography where I am exploring a region and am not entirely sure where I am going until an image is found and made. Then I know why I came. After making this photograph of one of my favourite staircases, I chose to investigate where it led to. I reached the first corner and taking a few steps further, looked up to find that it led nowhere but the sky. I was happy with that.

# Palazzo Giovanelli, Venice

## Italy

Film **Fuji 50asa**
Camera **Hasselblad 6cmx6cm**
Lens **40mm**
Exposure **15 secs f.22**
Filters **Polarizer**

For reasons I have never been able to fathom, as well as avenues of trees, I also have a great passion for staircases. I am sure there are many who share my fondness for flights of steps. Surely every architect will try to squeeze a fine staircase somewhere into the plans. The great set designers of Rank, Universal or 20th Century Fox films offered us some of the most wonderful staircases ever known in the iconographic movies of the thirties and forties. I am reminded of one in particular, where the indefatigable Bette Davies steps, not altogether confidently, down a staircase in some studio lot, muttering something about seat belts and bumpy nights.

But the staircase is more than just about the practicalities of getting up to the next floor: a staircase is symbolic, it is about ascending, about getting higher. In those self-same movies, the famous monologues delivered by the protagonist to the lesser mortals quivering in expectation below, were towering in their weighty power; it was the staircase and its elevation that provided the star with the oomph.

Perhaps my affection for the staircase comes from my family home in southern England. My regular night-time dream flights from the top to the bottom of our staircase were faultless. No crash landings for me but a perfect touchdown, like a feather dropping delicately to the floor. A staircase has featured in a number of images that I have made and there is never a time when I do not go in search of one.

Some years ago, I was working on a book on Venice. Being inquisitive, I pushed open a door into an indoor courtyard, to reveal the Palazzo Giovanelli. It was something akin to walking straight into an operatic set in La Scala, Milan: there were mosaics,wrought iron, scrolled pillars, arches, sculptures and the staircase with a delicious band of highlight at the end of each tread. A large cracked skylight allowed rain to fall onto this elaborate tableau, but the light from above was just what I needed to illuminate the star-shaped pattern at the centre of my photograph.

Everything seemed almost perfect: the pink of the marble, the mysterious green alcove half way up the stairs which appeared to have no purpose, and the carved motifs at the top of the two arch designs under the steps, one sadly broken.

The light level was low but one of the great pleasures of photography is the knowledge that an image can be made with a minimal amount of light. A familiar combination of shutter speed and aperture may be something like ⅟125 of a second at f.8 – yet here, I was happily working at 15 seconds at f.22.

I found it strangely hard to leave this place. All the components seemed to interlock so well, and for a fleeting moment I did wonder if I might see Bette dressed in flowing red velvet descending the staircase. But this was real Venice, not make believe Hollywood.

# Palazzo Vergottini, Lombardy
## Italy

Film **Fuji Velvia**
Camera **Hasselblad 6cm x 6cm**
Lens **50mm**
Exposure **1sec f.22**

I have always loved the theatre. I am unfailingly thrilled to find myself 'taken in' to the very essence of a play, not necessarily by the actors, but by the unsung heroes of the piece, the lighting director and the set designer. They too contribute very significantly to the success of the play; their work can bring a play to life.

I could so easily have missed Palazzo Vergottini. Like the mathematics department of Siena University (page 74), I had wondered what lay beyond the giant oak door, and when I inquisitively pushed it open, one of the finest theatrical set pieces I have seen in nearly thirty years of photography was revealed. At any moment, I imagined, I may see Juliet in her nightdress, arms outstretched, beseeching Romeo to remain.

I am ambivalent about architectural images, as I feel that I am merely recording the work of the architect. He is responsible for design, balance and cohesion, while I have merely made a transparency from the appropriate angle using the light which shows the building at its best. Much as I admire the highly specialized architectural photographer, for me there is too little latitude for self-expression.

Everything about this theatrical set was right: the broad steps in the foreground and the secondary steps behind; the six faces of walls with the seventh to the right slightly hidden; the crusty stuccowork of the terracotta walls so typical of Italy: the chunky sculptured balustrades, the shuttered windows, the balconies, the worn stone slabs set diagonally into the quadrant and the disappearing alleyway beyond, with the lamp encouraging the eye to wander through. I wanted to shake the hand of this set designer. It was a masterpiece.

I could not conceive that this might be private property and that photography was forbidden. That would be like winning the lottery and finding the ticket was invalid. I had no choice but to make an image of this place.

I prepared the camera, set it on the tripod and waited for the light to soften. There had been a splash of sunlight but that was not for me. I did not want any increased contrast, for the precious alleyway at the back of the image would have been lost. Thankfully, only one person appeared. She was wearing a brightly coloured headscarf and was striding purposefully towards the steps. At the end of the hour that I had been there, waiting for the sun to drop, or disappear behind a cloud, the headscarf lady reappeared, laughing. In place of the scarf, she was sporting a fine coiffure. I was rather disappointed to learn that to the left of this photograph there was a hairdressing salon and that the lady had just gone in for a hairdo. After she had gone, I was alone, finding it difficult to leave. I had fallen hopelessly in love with this place. Surprisingly, Juliet never appeared.

Palazzo Vergottini, Lombardy, Italy

# Corfu
## Greece

Film **Fuji Velvia**
Camera **Hasselblad 6cmx6cm**
Lens **50mm**
Exposure **1/15th f.11**
Filters **ND 2 stop graduated**

Those who have visited Corfu will no doubt have their preference for the inland or for the coast. In high summer an aerial view of this lovely island would reveal thousands of shiny roofs and hundreds of thousands of human bodies lying prostrate and motionless. A visitor from another planet would be bewildered by such a display. I stood in the rain on the southern tip, pondering all of this, and contemplating what could possibly be done here.

In our respective summers, our mass migration to the fringes of our countries is perhaps more than just frolicking in the sea and turning our skins to deep amber. At the edge of land where sand or pebbles mark the foreground we see three rectangles of sky, sea and land often in equal proportions. There is much comfort to be had from these simple shapes. Looking out across an ocean can often bring an immediate calming of the mind, a subduing of racing thoughts. Perhaps, like staring into the heart of a candle flame, the mind can contemplate lofty notions of existence and purpose as we gaze out questioningly to the horizon. Freya Stark said in her book *Perseus to the Wind*: 'and if one asked which of all sights in nature is most lastingly satisfying, would one not choose the horizon?'

In the rain I indulged in none of these meditations, but simply felt frustration as to what, if anything, might be achieved. Often food and refreshment are of no consequence when images are being made, but here in rain-sodden Corfu, I became desperate for food. With that in mind, I turned to leave and walk up the beach, only to be greeted, in the far distance, by a band of cornflower blue. With a northerly wind, I hoped that within an hour or so, the sun would be unmasked by the rain clouds, and the shoreline lit. I miscalculated. The wind speeds above us are, of course, greater than at ground level and within 20 minutes the division between blue and deep grey was both more pronounced and nearer to where I stood. There had been one further heavy burst of rain which had forced me to shelter under a leaky and ineffective tarpaulin, and with the passing of the rain I was offered the very light I had hoped for. With not a molecule of dust in the air, the hard sunlight smashed onto the near water, filling it with an opaline iridescence. Setting this outrageous green against the distant foreboding rain-clouds was obviously the thing to do. As I look again at this image, I wonder whether others looking at it feel that the storm is brewing, soon to arrive, or that it has passed. Depending on the outlook of the individual, perhaps it is a case of the vessel being half full or half empty. The anticipated glass of good Greek wine in a nearby taverna quickly dismissed the idea of any glass being empty.

# Lake Titicaca

## Bolivia

Some years ago, I was panting my way through the streets of La Paz, trying to shake off altitude sickness and acclimatize to the thin air. After a day or two, we were off to what is arguably regarded as the finest lake in the world, Lake Titicaca. I thought I had seen true azure in parts of the Adriatic, Aegean and Caribbean, but looking at Lake Titicaca was like staring into the heart of a vast sapphire.

I had taken a boat to an island in the middle of the lake, where I discovered a primitive settlement of a couple of houses and a wooden shack for a school.

Film **Fuji Provia**
Camera **Fuji 6cmx 17cm**
Lens **300mm**
Exposure **1/8th f 32**
Filters **Polarizer**

I begged the teacher to let me have two desks to stand on. It was crucial to have height. There were two pinnacles with which I had become obsessed: the top of the sail of the fast-moving boat, and the apex of the thatched construction. I was determined that the image could only work if I could drop these two points under the distant mountain range. The battered school desks did the trick and I stood, somewhat precariously, and by a mere millimetre, triumphant!

It was cold but I was on fire with excitement as I saw the image taking shape. The serenity which I hope this image conveys, was in fact born in a climate of frenzy; if I could, I would always carry a sapphire in my pocket to remind me of this extraordinary convergence of events; but then I suppose I have the photograph…that will do.

# Miroir de Scey
## France

Film **Fuji 50asa**
Camera **Hasselblad 6cmx6cm**
Lens **50mm**
Exposure **3 secs f.22**

Water again. Perhaps we are drawn to water because we can have no ownership over it but we feel able to claim it – for the time that we are there – as truly ours. At the seaside, the area of sea that we float in is for that time our patch, our very own. Water is too quicksilver in nature for anyone to claim territorial rights to it. Riparian ownership for the fisherman is not the same thing.

I had been feeling a bit under the weather, and was preparing to head north back up through five hundred miles of this fine country to Le Havre and home. Then the gift was suddenly there at the side of the road; there was the little Miroir de Scey glimpsed for a millisecond through thick bushes. In France it is still possible to travel along a very minor road almost entirely alone, so it was easy to stop, and investigate. I scrambled down a muddy bank, and there was this secret place. In my head, I sensed that the image had been made already; now I just had to get all of it onto a piece of film, if I could. That trial and error approach stayed with me for many years, never feeling confident enough to know whether what I saw would make an image. Would I ever learn to tell the difference? Surely we must be able to define our objective before embarking on the production.

The camera, its functions, its operation are all equally scientific, yet what is transmitted through the optics is essentially subjective. It carries with it an emotional response to what has been seen, coupled with a wished-for evocation of the experience, none of which may convert into an image that successfully conveys the photographer's artistic and expressive intention.

This latter aspect of photography is often whimsical, exploratory, vulnerable to both a misjudgement of aesthetic merit and a misreading of dynamics that were thought to be fully evident at the time, yet are not present in the final image. The entire process is subject to deviation of many kinds. When the transparency is seen on the light box, and the lack of magic is painfully missing, the disappointment can be agonizing as you realize that the image patently 'did not work'.

This is why compromise should be avoided at all costs. If the objective is clear, then compromise is out. Many a photographer will admit to having compromised, but a sense of self-betrayal is inescapable, and painfully remembered each time he looks at the image. Like the actor whose stage performance was below par on the day it was filmed, there will be nothing he or she can do. But they would know. No matter how fervent the acclaim, they will always know the truth.

With this intimate and gentle scene I hoped that what I saw and felt would be what I would see and feel again when I saw the resulting image of this modest little mill. Thankfully, at least for me, this was the case.

# Mopti

## Mali

Film **Kodak T400CN**
Camera **Hasselblad 6cmx6cm**
Lens **50mm**
Exposure **125th sec f.16**
Filters **Orange filter**

I had been asked to go to Timbuktu by Simon, an imaginative and creative businessman who has made it possible for me to see and photograph many wonderful places in the world. I shall be eternally indebted to him.

Looking at this photograph of the fisherman casting his net brings back memories of joy but also pain. The plan was to try to record this extraordinarily haphazard yet effective technique of fishing on the River Niger in Mopti, Mali.

Even with a good friend of mine relaying my positioning instructions to our boatman, I doubted that it would be possible to co-ordinate the correct camera position with that of the fisherman. Unlike a relatively static landscape, this was bordering on the chaotic. Both our boat and the fisherman's were very unstable. But we persevered, and with the sixth attempt, I hoped that we had made the image.

This was the fisherman's ballet. The preparation required the concentration of a star golfer, a barefoot waddle on the small platform to be assured of grip and balance, a steely look ahead, a magical five second moment of absolute stillness before committing to the act, and then with the combined style of a discus and javelin thrower, the final decision. The net was cast.

On this occasion, in one terrifyingly anxious moment as the great canopy flew above me, the fisherman wobbled just as the discus thrower does, to stop himself from crossing the line. He miraculously saved himself from falling into my arms. My finger pressed the shutter release. But what image was made?

On looking at the contact sheet, though, this was clearly the one. I could never have known that the central knot of the net would have been so perfectly in line with his left hand, that his outstretched right hand was just separated by the cuff of his gown, defining his hand as a hand and not a black lump, that his right foot did not quite mask his left, that the high clouds would be of just the correct character to ensure cohesion, and that the man steering the boat would balance so well with the fisherman. As I looked at the final print and saw the evidence of these crucial elements interlocking so beautifully, they all added up to a photographic miracle which seemed to have been governed by something else. But there was more. The ribbons of light within the net gave me much pleasure, especially along the top where the mesh was evident and where the rapid unfurling took place.

The entire circumference of the net was weighted with lead and on each previous attempt to make the image work, it hit me fairly and squarely on the top of my head. It was painful but the image had to be fought for, and looking at the finished print in the darkroom, I can not help but wonder what might have happened if my ballerina fisherman had fallen on top of me – it was a close thing.

# Vermont
## USA

Film **Fuji 100asa**
Camera **Hasselblad 6cmx6cm**
Lens **150mm**
Exposure **1/4 sec f.22-f.32**
Filters **81C filter**

The fact that I made this image at all should be attributed to my friend and distinguished photographer Clive Minnitt.

Towards the end of 1999, I travelled with a group of photographers to Vermont. In the fall, visitors flock to Maine, New Hampshire and Vermont. Like us, they come to see what is arguably the finest display of autumn colour in the world. From the lightest of yellows to deep maple red, the landscape's natural colour can overwhelm you – sometimes.

A year before the planned visit, I had made the travel arrangements. At the time, it was impossible to predict precisely when the maple leaves would be on fire, with the canary yellow silver birch leaves sizzling against the deep blue October sky.

As it was, we had been in Montpelier, our base, for a week, with the longed-for light continually eluding us. The hotel reception television, permanently tuned to the weather channel, taunted us with a depressing map of the locality. Above the north-east corner of the state was a repeating vortex of churning grey sludge. It was a low that was to persist for the entire week, with the same image every morning. Grey inside and out. The weather people had been infuriatingly right.

On the third morning, emerging from our hotel, we were met by a local landscape photographer. He told us that, same time last year, the colours and light were the best in twenty years of photography and that this year was the worst in living memory. It's odd how some folk seem to relish delivering bad news.

Despite a few heavy hearts, there was the usual bonhomie that you find in a small group of landscape photographers. At a bend in the road, Clive suddenly shouted out 'Stop!' by a vast array of pumpkins. I saw nothing immediately appealing about these bulbous fruits laid out across the damp landscape. But there was the tree with its deep orange canopy of leaves, and behind were the tattered stalks of maize, still upright and in orderly lines. In no time, each photographer had fallen to his knees with his camera, as if in some sort of ritualistic pumpkin worship.

Through the lens, I attempted to draw together pumpkins, leaves and corn, and when, finally, the image took shape, I sang out my thanks to Clive. The key here was to be low, but not so low that the tumble of pumpkins masked the base of the corn. Everything in the viewfinder was vivid orange but to ensure unity, I introduced a mild 81B amber filter to give an additional wash of warmth over the entire tableau.

As we left the US, we took off into a clear, star-filled night sky. Back home, an email arrived from a certain photographer, describing the glorious sunshine he had enjoyed the week after our stay. I took another look at my pumpkins on the light box and decided to pass on pumpkin soup for supper that night.

# Champagne
## France

Film **Fuji Velvia**
Camera **Hasselblad 6cmx6cm**
Lens **150mm**
Exposure **½ sec f.22-f.32**

In the autumn of 1999 I had returned from two weeks work in India. It was my first trip there, because, unlike my contemporaries in the late sixties and seventies, I had chosen (now with some regret) not to travel in pursuit of Maharishi Mahesh Yogi or to the ashrams of Rajasthan for meditation. This first visit to India had a disturbing effect on me. I had not been prepared to see humanity on such a vast scale, nor in such contrast to my known world. On my return, I found that I was unable to settle down and so, in search of some autumn colours, I crossed the channel bound for Epernay, the champagne grape-growing area of France.

The picking had taken place in the third week of October and, within a few days, I realized that once again I had misjudged the moment when the leaves would change. On the third day, despite fair and unseasonably warm weather, I chose to head home. With the car packed and feeling mildly despondent, I drove towards Le Havre, leaving Epernay and its bubbly behind me. Within fifteen minutes, about a kilometre beyond me, I noticed a double line of fine plane trees, the lower half of their trunks half-hidden by the stubbled slope of a nearby hill. After some dead ends and a chain-barrier deftly lifted out of the way, I was able to find what remains of one of the most glorious plane tree avenues I have seen.

What is it about a tree-lined avenue that holds so much appeal? Surely, it is the uncertainty and mystery of what lies beyond. This avenue near Epernay needed light to introduce a sparkle and to enliven the trees with some speckled highlights. That afternoon there seemed little prospect of light, but I still set up the tripod.

As I was preparing to refine things, I heard the familiar sound of a 2CV. I had hoped that I might be alone that early afternoon, but alas, the flimsy door of the car slammed shut followed by the falling latch of the same gate that I had walked through. Within a minute or two a middle-aged man dressed incongruously in a tailored suit was standing by my side. 'You are photographing my trees,' he said in perfect English. I launched into all sorts of explanations as to why I was here, none of them necessary. I apologized for trespassing (which I had felt I was not), and with a grin he explained that he lived 20 miles from this spot. 'I am an enthusiastic amateur photographer, and for the last twenty years I have been passing these trees on my way to work, and every time I pass them, I say to myself that I must make a photograph of these trees.' Now I was beginning to understand. With a hint of feigned resentment, he went on: 'So, now I see that a bloody Englishman is photographing my trees!' We laughed together, he walked back to his car, the sun shone, I made my photograph and we both left the trees to themselves.

# Lucca, Tuscany
## Italy

Film **Fuji Velvia**
Camera **Hasselblad 6cmx6cm**
Lens **150mm**
Exposure **2 seconds f.32**
Filters **81B**

The impulse to make an image of an arcade or cloister probably comes from the same desire that I have to put the camera to my eye for an avenue of trees. Perhaps it satisfies a sense of order, the pleasure to be had from repetition, the pleasing aesthetics of arcs and diagonals: who knows? But I will always remember the happy and yet frustrating time spent in the elegant town of Lucca. Florence and Siena are often sited as the jewels of Tuscany, but Lucca should not be overlooked. Many a day have I spent there, wandering within its Renaissance walls. For the lover of architectural detail, there is a feast of opportunities: the fine Romanesque cathedral, palaces, squares and the arcaded cloisters abutting the main square.

It is not always the case that an image has to be awaited and received; sometimes it is blatantly 'for sale' and shouts out to be acquired. The lemon diagonal sunlight bands, fat towards the beginning of the image and skinny at the far end, were irresistible to me, and the bicycle parked nonchalantly and set so perfectly two thirds of the way down the twenty or so arches sent me into photographic rapture. I did not know at the time that when a print was made, the bands of sunlight would create the optical illusion of steps in the front of the image.

Within minutes, I had set up. This was not the time for sedate photography where waiting is the game; this was about urgency, about grasping opportunities. I could not bear the prospect of the sun slipping behind a cloud – perhaps a cloud that was so vast, so infinite there would be no sun on my arcade for a week, for a month or year. I could hear the sirens screeching in my mind. This was panic time.

I had never suspected that I would be undone by the mischievous but infuriating little ten-year-old lad who was determined to taunt me by slipping in and out of each arch one by one, always managing to pre-empt the moment when I would depress the shutter of my camera. In normal circumstances I am able to cast an eye upward to see the state of play with sun and clouds, but here I was unable to know if I was to be denied my light and, if so, when. Would it be in a moment, or could I relax in the knowledge that I would be afforded at least ten minutes of direct undiffused sunlight? If I had known, then I would have had the luxury of being able to join in with my little friend Luccio and buffoon with him for a while. But it was too risky. Supposing I were to have stepped away from the camera to glance at the sky for just a few seconds. That may have been the moment when he too was distracted and I could have made my exposure.

Finally a pleading call from his mother brought this cat and mouse game to a conclusion, but not before he peeped around the far pillar at the end of the arcade to snub me at the last. Game set and match to me…just.

# Cantabria
## Spain

Film **Fuji 50asa**
Camera **Hasselblad 6cmx6cm**
Lens **250mm**
Exposure **2 secs f.45**
Filters **Polarizer**

There are times, after prolonged rain, when despair sets in and the whole idea of further photography seems unlikely and unwelcome. I had been working on a book on Spain and, after perhaps three to four weeks, I was becoming creatively exhausted. The only thing to do was head for home and see if I could catch an early boat from Santander on the north-west coast of the country. Despite my affection for Spain, the prospect of returning to the UK was very inviting.

Yet to leave these gentle mountain ranges of the Picos de Europa and the fast-flowing rivers that weave through their slopes seemed madness. I decided to stay a further day: if the rain persisted, I would telephone the ferry company and leave.

The morning broke as it had done for the last four days, damp and without light. The sense of hopelessness was overwhelming and within an hour or so I had phoned and changed my departure time to that evening for the night crossing.

Almost as if to taunt me, the next bend revealed this image. Here the saturated green was to do the work. In the flattest of light with no sunlight at all – not even a whiff of brightness in any direction – and no competing greens to steal the eye away from the precious triangle two thirds of the way up the image, this tableau was delivered to me on the proverbial plate.

The bracken, which dominated the image, was crucial to act as a foil for the green slash, and the russet folds lying diagonally across the square lend an order to things. I remember seeing the haystacks and the untidy bits that often accompany a farmyard, and then the cherry on the cake: the red tiled roof of the very plain farmhouse. This vivid, almost fluorescent red roof played the most crucial part. It acted as a bright beacon to which the eye is drawn and anchored. If the roof had been dark grey, would I have seen this image? What did I see first, the red roof or the green? I enjoy posing these questions but I suspect I saw the two together.

Thankfully the surrounding trees would have lost all their leaves some weeks before. Had they not, then other splashes of colour might have interfered with the two central characters of green and red.

From a mood of descending melancholia to photographic ecstasy – and all in the time it takes to go round the bend.

# The Manger, Berkshire
## England

Film **Kodak Ektachrome 64asa**
Camera **Hasselblad 6cmx6cm**
Lens **50mm**
Exposure **¼ f.22**
Filters **ND 2 stop graduated**

Whenever I look at this photograph I remember having a great urge to roll up in a ball and tumble and bowl down this combe, arriving no doubt giggling and hysterical at the end. Many a child must have done so, and on the day that I was here I was tempted. The manger remains one of my favourite images for this, plus the sky, the cloud shadow and the light.

There are two features here that play a role so important that without them the photograph would be diminished, perhaps never made. The sliver of light on the leading finger of land supports the other beyond. Even such a small amount of light breathes life into this side of the image. The manger has a voluptuousness to it that cannot fail to seduce the eye. In the distance the land appears smooth and newly shaven; in the foreground, information is given on the tuftyness of the grass. I like the sprinkling of green and yellow, making a palette of two shades that weave in and out of each other, while the sheep tracks act like rows of seating in an amphitheatre.

Of course, the painter or photographer of the landscape would be preoccupied with light and its distribution throughout the image. I was brought up on shadow detail and whilst it is not always possible to ensure its evidence, I always look for it. I was thankful for the pale nature of the slope in shadow to the left, enjoying the light being reflected back, both from its own light surface, and from its neighbour opposite, acting as a giant reflector.

How fortunate I was for the sky to be so supportive of my intention. I had no desire to reveal to the spectator the featureless flat land beyond. This would have stolen the eye away from where I wanted it to reside: in the great bowl and not beyond. With my antennae up and alert, and with light and shade constantly dancing through the landscape, the atmosphere was one of acute anticipation. At a given moment the friendly and compliant cloud, not particularly spectacular in itself, provided me with an almost entire cloak of shadow to be draped over the flat land in the distance. There is a minute band of light land in the far distance but it is too far to be obtrusive. The action has been preserved in the foreground and when the cloud shadow to the left had uncovered the far slope of the manger, lighting it softly, I felt ready to commit to the modest act of depressing the shutter.

The manger brings with it a sense of satisfaction similar to the photograph of the Embalse de Yelsa near Pamplona (page 106). Of course all images by their nature will present a sense of stillness, but the manger conveys a silence to me that is as strong as any other in this book.

Everything is curved and rhythmic in this photograph. Scoops, s-shapes, swells and softness. Little wonder that I wanted to roll through it all.

# Chicklade, Wiltshire
## England

Film **Fuji Velvia**
Camera **Hasselblad 6cmx6cm**
Lens **150mm**
Exposure **1/4 sec f.22**
Filters **ND 1.5 stop graduated and Polarizer**

On a June morning, I was heading reluctantly for London on another business trip. Heavy rain was forecast, and I wondered, as many landscape photographers do, whether or not to take my camera with me. But it is never the case of taking 'just a camera'. If an image is to be made, all filters, lenses, tripod and ladder must be taken. It's an 'all or nothing' business. Everything must be available in preparation for the surprise image that may present itself.

As I drove due east towards London, the rain was throwing up so much spray that I was unable to see the landscape to my left. I could never have known that on my return, I would discover a combination of colour and line that would satisfy me for many years to come.

To be on the cusp of bad weather receding, and good weather arriving (whatever bad or good weather means), often ensures a sharpness to the air. All the floating dust has been driven down with the rain, allowing undiffused sunlight to flood across the landscape.

The north-westerly (how often one hears mariners speak of this troublesome wind) which had brought the driving rain to accompany my easterly journey was to greet me with fairer weather on my return that afternoon.

It was an electrifying moment, which appeared to have materialized once again for me and me alone. The farmer responsible for this astonishing juxtaposition of colours, found me on the fourth step of my ladder. Approaching me as if it was entirely normal to be standing on a stepladder in the middle of the Wiltshire countryside, he observed that I would be unlikely ever to see anything quite like this again. 'I planted my rape too late,' he said. 'Oilseed rape – the yellow one – is an early spring crop and linseed a late spring/early summer one. You have benefited from my error.' In a state of pure photographic rapture, I motioned to the line of the wall delineating the division of the two crops, and the minute splash of bright light far beyond in the distance, thankful that it activated this part of the image, lending much sought-after depth. We discussed the heavy monochrome cloud which was full of foreboding, and I wondered whether this image with the pulsating tension between the blue and the yellow would appear too gaudy, too psychedelic, just simply too unbelievable. 'People may not believe this image,' I said to my farmer friend. 'I will testify," he said. 'I will bear witness.'

# Almond Blossom, Alpujarras
## Spain

For twenty years I had been waiting for an opportunity to see the almond blossom in the mountainous Alpujarras, in Southern Spain. The time that the trees decide to blossom is unpredictable but friends in Andalucia had promised to contact me as soon as the time was right and I was now settled with my camera in a light pink explosion of a million petals.

The almond is a humble little tree. It has not the gnarled, lived-in look of an Umbrian olive, nor the sturdiness of a Dordogne walnut. But for ten days of the year around St Valentine's day, the almond tree cocks a snook at all the other trees around. It transforms itself along with its thousands of neighbours, into a member of the most beautifully costumed corps de ballet in the world. For ten days only, the landscape turns milky pink: this was what I had come for, and on 14 February 2002 I fell in love with the almond tree. To be on an Andalucian hill-side, smothered by almond blossom, seemed to me as good as life can get.

However, none of the possible images I saw matched the preconceived idea that was rooted in my imagination: an image created in my mind's eye, even before leaving the UK. Nothing here stirred me; it would not translate from three dimensions into two, despite its loveliness.

From the roadside a path led up to a small hill covered with a profusion of almond blossom. But I could not make anything work. Too many trees masked each other, while shadows from each adjacent tree cast muddled, secondary shadows onto its neighbour; there needed to be some degree of separation, some legibility. But on my way back downhill, I saw the image that had been awaiting me all the time. Each tree was nicely delineated, with dark brown trunks, the blossom at its peak, and a perfect shade of cornflower blue above.

I am not fond of cropping so radically that branches have to be sacrificed on the sides of the frame if there is no compositional reason to do so. Here, it was the foreground four that held everything in check. Their trunks, their unmasked clear coherence gave me the confidence to go ahead and make the image. I could see the point at which the tree emerges from the ground, and that mattered to me.

Some months later a gentleman visiting a gallery where this image was hung asked me if I knew the old Islamic proverb about the almond tree; I did not. 'May I tell you?' he said. 'Please do,' I replied, wondering if his story would be long and abstract. With a benign expression he said: 'A man approached the almond tree and asked the almond tree, "Speak to me of God," … and the almond tree blossomed.'

Film **Fuji Velvia**
Camera **Hasselblad 6cmx6cm**
Lens **250mm**
Exposure **1 sec f.45**
Filters **Polarizer**

Almond Blossom, Alpujarras, Spain 

# Sélestat, Bas-Rhin

## France

Film **Fuji 50asa**
Camera **Hasselblad 6cmx6cm**
Lens **50mm**
Exposure **1 sec f.22**
Filters **81B**

The Route du Vin from Colmar towards Strasbourg is always an enjoyable drive. With the mighty Rhine just twenty kilometres away, this is a landscape of semi-timbered houses, dilapidated castles, medieval villages and the ubiquitous vine.

Winter is perhaps the best time for landscape photography in northern Europe; not for snow and ice particularly, and certainly not for the cold, but for the unique quality of light that sometimes graces the landscape. A vast tract of land, seemingly flat and without undulation, can reveal, in a low oblique light, an unexpected rippling blanket of form.

Normally I would wish for a sky that lent drama to my image, such as a fine dusting of high cirrus cloud; but on this occasion any such sky would have been an interference, a distraction from the symmetry and order here.

I am always concerned about the general arrangement of shapes controlling the structure of the image. In fact, there is an element that destabilizes this image, and although some might suggest that it introduces a sense of depth, it seems too weak to do so. It is the line of reeds bisecting the frame almost precisely in half. But thankfully, their presence is barely evident as their own reflection merges into those of the stately trees. Ideally, I would have preferred it if there had been no spit of land as we see here, and perhaps the surface area of the sky above could equate to its reflection below.

The deep magenta hills beyond and the reflection of the trees become softened by the mildest of breezes across the water. This landscape evokes a sensation of stillness and serenity. It is barely possible to imagine the evening rush hour traffic of some sixty cars a minute racing along the busy road less than fifty metres behind me.

# Islay, Inner Hebrides
## Scotland

Film **Fuji 50asa**
Camera **Hasselblad 6cmx6cm**
Lens **40mm**
Exposure **2 sec f.22**
Filters **Polarizer**

If I had arrived on Islay, the southernmost island of the Inner Hebrides six thousand five hundred years ago, I would have been wandering through great forests, but in 1998 my partiality to trees was not to be satisfied. There were few to be seen.

In the winter of that year, I spent many happy hours near Bowmore on the southern shore of Loch Indaal. I have some good and amusing memories of this special island, one being a rather alarming incident when I was chased by a swan in Claggain Bay. I had been quietly making an image of grey skies and muted coloured pebbles in the foreground with a solitary lone swan in the distance. With no warning, the swan drew its mighty wings back and with a dreadful howling sound flew up the beach and within a few seconds was confronting me face to face. I had never before been chased by a swan, flying at one metre above the ground, neck outstretched and eyes fixed on me. Nor, thankfully, has it happened since. It was a dramatic and frightening experience. Within a second or two I had collected my camera and I was away and on the road to Bowmore for this photograph, which was made in the evening of that same day. The image here is something of a contrast to the previous one. I have never understood what provoked that swan.

Everything appeared to be right about this place. The boat was traditional, nothing was obtrusive, all was sublimely at rest. No rush to reach for the camera: time to drink in and absorb. I was disturbed for some time about the froth in the immediate foreground and wondered whether I should crop the image – not into a panoramic, as I have done once before, but into a rectangle, a format more traditional for landscape photography. This would produce a sliver of water sitting beneath the boat, with the vast sky above. However, despite the merits of such cropping, I remained loyal to the square.

I do not normally use extreme wide-angle or excessively long lenses and am quite content to work with just four fixed focal length lenses from mild wide to mild long. If an image betrays which lens has been used, that can be intrusive to both its meaning and what to understand from it.

For me, no other place so personifies calm. The isolation of the small dinghy suggests vulnerability and solitude. The canopy of broken magenta cloud dropping little pale puffballs of reflection across the water's surface pleases me. I can enjoy this image for its utter simplicity, and for perhaps the oddest of reasons: the bow of the boat points away and upward to the distance.

If I were to return to this place I would hope to find this modest little clinker – built dinghy in the same place; I could not bear to think it would ever go anywhere.

# The Borders
## Scotland

Film **Agfa 1000 asa**
Camera **Hasselblad 6cmx6cm**
Lens **150mm**
Exposure **1/125th f.32**

There are two people in my family who feel strongly about this image; one likes it very much, the other detests it. Obviously I side with the one who likes it, who says it is contemporary. It ascends, therefore I personally was bound to like it.

I had been travelling in the Border country and from a busy road I saw this post and rail fence and was immediately compelled to turn round and retrace my steps. It did occur to me at the time that there may be a few folk who would be bewildered at my turning and driving back some three miles to visit a fence. Once again, I wondered whether what I had seen in a millisecond had been embellished by my overactive imagination. It had not and I was so pleased to have returned. I was struck by the measurements that would have been needed to cut and set the posts into the ground with such precision; each pointed and driven to a particular depth. This was art. No need for me to confirm it with a photograph.

This fence was so much more than a mere structure. It was a masterpiece. I wished to meet the man who made this work, to encourage him to talk me through it, to acquaint me with every hazard, every joy of its construction and to know something of his elation at the end of his toils. Like the autumn ploughman looking back at his furrows so accurately aligned, there is pleasure in accuracy.

So often, especially in the western world, we credit and acclaim individuals who have made great achievements. Had I the authority to bestow an honour on the shoulders of the man who made this fence, I would have done so; such was my admiration for him and his skill. No doubt he would have wished to do the same for the men who hewed and fashioned the rock to build a thousand miles of dry-stone walls in Yorkshire and Cumbria. They were all artists.

Once there was a type of film available with a dedicated speed of one thousand asa. It had certain applications and its boast was grain and accordingly low contrast. Like many I cared for it deeply. Sadly, it was withdrawn, but a few months beforehand, a photographer friend in the USA panicked and acquired a thousand rolls, such was his addiction.

I had not wanted to use a fine-grain film here. The wooden fence I felt should not appear too invasive upon the land. I hoped that the coarseness of the film would unify fence, hill and grass. The wood of the fence had weathered, and its warm silvery grey sat well on the slope of the November grass. Thankfully, there was no vivid blue in the sky to conflict with the browns and steely greys.

I still do not understand why I care so much for that part of the fence that crawls its way over the top of the slope seemingly escaping from something. No doubt there is some explanation, but I hoped this lovely thing might have no end.

# Camargue, Provence
## France

Film **Fuji 50asa**
Camera **Hasselblad 6cmx6cm**
Lens **50mm**
Exposure **½sec f.22**
Filters **Polarizer**

I had wanted to visit this region of southern France for many years and when I was fortunate enough to be given a commission to produce a book on Provence, I knew that it would involve a visit to the Camargue.

Like Venice and other iconographic places, the Camargue conjured up visions of squadrons of flamingoes and the flowing manes of the famous white feral horses. This landscape is just a few metres above sea level and is bisected by a thousand waterways like a child's cat's cradle, every one splitting the landscape into rectangles and triangles. The Camargue is more about water than land, and I was happy here.

The Rhône pours itself into the Mediterranean at Port de Fos; an ignominious end for such a noble river with a few thousand kilometres of experience behind it, to finish its journey in such a hideous sprawling industrial zone.

But away from tankers and cranes are the reeds. There is a corner in my heart for the reed, with its furry flags flying from rod-straight stalks. The receding nature of this golden triangle is what here causes a further triangle to emerge, below and to the right. Infact, I well remember trying to make the image comply to give me three perfect triangles. It became exasperating. This was not a photograph intended to create an emotional tug, there was nothing more here than the reeds, the sky and the reflection, and yet, fond of this image as I am, I remain saddened by the sky.

It could have been so much better. I had seen the high cirrus, which, at nearly ten kilometres in altitude is made up of ice crystals sweeping through the high troposphere. I could see my favourite clouds racing south, out and away from my square. I had underestimated the wind speeds at this altitude and in the two minutes that it took for me to set up, everything had changed. By the time I was in place, with swarms of mosquitoes to accompany me, there were mere remnants left of the phantom-like cirrus to place above the reeds.

In their place, I was offered a gaping hole of indigo blue, further accentuated by the polarising filter that I had neglected to remove.

Had I been just three minutes earlier, the wispy clouds above would have linked with the feathery reeds below and a happy marriage would have been established. This relationship which was so obvious to the eye was to be denied me, as the clouds in this image are neither sufficient in number nor surface area.

I remember being broken-hearted by the sense of loss of what might have been. A friend later suggested that with some digital manipulation I could have my clouds back. That may be so, but would I have slept at night? And anyway is it not in the nature of phantoms to vanish almost before they have been glimpsed?

# The Somme
## France

Film **Fuji Velvia**
Camera **Hasselblad 6cmx6cm**
Lens **50mm**
Exposure **½ sec f.22**

It was in early January of 2002 that this image was made in the Somme, near the Western Front. In winter there can be few places in the world that have such resonance. It is, in the main, a flat featureless landscape with nothing like the number of visitors who go further south for the sun. Those who do visit the Somme go for essentially one reason: remembrance.

I planned to see some of the war cemeteries where many thousands of young soldiers lie. In these places, numbers take on a new meaning as you contemplate row after row of carefully tended graves. It is a salutary and necessary experience.

Being inquisitive, I am often drawn to explore roads that appear to go nowhere. On one such foray, I found this stand of poplars. For the right elevation I needed the small stepladder, as I did not wish the tops of the marsh reeds to interfere with the middle part of the trunks. Eight feet high did the trick, and there I stood in the cold bleak air of the Somme in January, hands in pockets waiting for some light. None came, but my reliable friend, the BBC World Service, kept me company until at dusk, I returned to the hotel. I knew what quality of light I was waiting for, and from what direction and how widespread it needed to be, but for me that is an accepted part of the procedure. This wished-for light may not materialize, but I always remain hopeful that light will arrive and unlock the image.

I could not now abandon these trees. They were almost friends. On my return the following day, there was a splash of late afternoon sunlight, but it did not travel all the way down the nave of what was becoming reminiscent of a great cathedral. The light that did materialize resulted in a half-lit scene: too diffuse and not sufficiently directional. So I spent the next four days waiting on my ladder for the ever-absent sun. But I was still perfectly content. I just wanted the light to sweep right through and up to the tops of the trees. I had one more day.

On the fifth afternoon at about 3.30, the light arrived. It performed perfectly, so that the almost vertical hill at the far end was dropped into shadow. The filigree branches at the very end of the nave were revealed, blocking any information. The slight breeze allowed the tops of the reeds to waft through the plantation.

The clouds above were of such shapes that the light falling into my 'cathedral' was of exactly the right amount, and in exactly the right place. The clouds had revealed the spirit of the place, and the longed-for illumination spread across the scene. It was a moving finale to the end of this cold January day. Not a soul was about. But there seemed to be thousands.

# Siena, Tuscany
## Italy

Landscape photography is often about a search of some kind and I have been rewarded by my curiosity. Here I chose to investigate the area around Siena cathedral. With the remarkable façade of the cathedral in view at the end of the street, I noticed a double-fronted door closed but for a small gap. With a light push, I entered what I was to learn was the mathematics department of Siena University.

I had planned that this austere tableau would lend itself to black and white and after half an hour or so, I was ready to make some exposures. Thick cloud above diffused the light a little more than I would have wished, with contrast accordingly being almost too minimal. I was thankful for the artificial light spilling through the lattice grill at the top of the staircase. It provided both an end to the staircase and also a welcoming brightness, suggesting continuation of some kind.

I became intrigued by the giant central hexagonal pillar. It was clearly of great structural importance, and yet it seemed to disrupt the continuity of the staircase. It related to the smaller perpendicular plinth on which the very grumpy lion sat, and of course the stone balustrades, but I wondered why it could not have been placed to the right allowing continuity of the three-sided staircase down to the floor. However, my main pleasure was in the stairs themselves and in the wonderful overall patina of the back wall and pillar, no doubt caused by damp and years of patching. The cloud gave way to a little diffused sun, raising contrast and providing deeper blacks and brighter whites. Things were looking good. No custodian approached me to hasten me from the university property and there were no other visitors.

I placed a roll of film into the camera and began an exposure with a small aperture and a long bulb shutter speed of some 60 seconds. Suddenly, the calm atmosphere was radically transformed. There was frantic alarmed shouting as a group of maths students, returning late to class, swept through the door, bounded up the staircase, and through the beautifully decorated doorway at the top. They were gone in just ten seconds. I chose to continue with the exposure.

One of the things I like most about photography is contemplating what may have taken place before or after the shutter was depressed and, in this case, during. For one sixth of the exposure, a gang of students had swept through, pummelling one another in their urgency to attain the lead. All this hysterical commotion was of no consequence, as five sixths of the exposure took place in the atmosphere of calm that prevailed before and after. I made a few further exposures, but as expected, when I looked at the roll of negative film, none of the frames showed any student activity.

Time and mathematics.

Film **Agfapan 25asa**
Camera **Hasselblad 6cmx6cm**
Lens **40mm**
Exposure **60secs f.22**

Siena, Tuscany, Italy

# San Gimignano, Tuscany
## Italy

Film **Fuji 50asa**
Camera **Hasselblad 6cmx6cm**
Lens **80mm**
Exposure **¼sec f.22**
Filters **ND 1 stop graduated and 81B**

It is not uncommon for me to take a fresh look at photographs that I have made, and from which, over time, I have become detached. Then I can see them with fresh eyes, as if for the first time, or even look upon them as if they were taken by someone else. But if, for some reason, I return to the place where the image was made, everything about the entire experience is evoked and made vivid. It is impossible to entirely wipe it from my memory.

I have visited and circumnavigated this extraordinary town many times, and each time I leave with the same feeling: that the landscape around San Gimignano, perhaps one of the top ten Tuscan destinations, is infinitely more interesting than the town itself. Everything in the landscape sweeps up to the settlement, all converging at a point as if vine tree and ear of corn are showing their allegiance to the town crowning the hill. This is quintessential Tuscan bucolic. With eyes half closed, I can see a medieval peasant farmer in coarse cloth hoeing the land and pruning the vine. Everything is in order for him. He has harvested his grapes, his bonfire consumes the waste and his land rests.

Over the years I have visited San Gimignano and am always intrigued to see the changes that a new year has brought. Once there were wooden stakes to support the vine at the end of the line. When I made this image, they had been replaced by moulded concrete. Thankfully those within the lines were mostly wooden. Wood and the grape seem more in keeping with one another but for the viticulturist who cares more for efficiency than looks, it must be concrete.

I have used an unobtrusive but effective light amber filter here to emphasize the yellow. When this photograph was made, it was not possible to use a filter that introduced warmth to a local area of the image; everything was warmed and what little blue prevailed was virtually eaten up by amber.

I made about six exposures of San Gimignano, and for the last, I changed the mild neutral density graduated filter to one that provided me with a stop more density for the sky. For some years, I would look at this transparency and consider the sky too dark. But now I believe this one is more representative of the sky that prevailed at the time. My eye could resolve the sky and its subtleties, but the film could not. The neutral density graduated filter put skies back where they belong.

I remained here for two hours or so; there seemed nowhere better to go. I felt that I could float and drift away with the smoke.

# San Quirico d'Orcia, Tuscany
## Italy

Film **Fuji Velvia**
Camera **Nikon 35mm**
Lens **28mm**
Exposure **1sec f.22**
Filters **Polarizer**

I cannot look at this image without remembering *Barry Lyndon*, a fine movie set in Ireland. The director of photography and the cinematographer together produced many lasting images of dark brooding skies and brilliantly lit foregrounds that still resonate in my mind. These presumably surprise conditions were offered to them and they capitalized on the remarkable lighting, which in turn breathed pathos into each scene. I stood in this field remembering that movie.

The whole business of 'hope' always intrigues me. Sometimes I find myself speaking out loud, rather more often than I care to reveal and generally my dialogue is with the sky, the clouds and of course the light. I became intimately acquainted with this dark cloud mass and its structure and, with rain pounding all around me, I hoped it would pass on to the south and drench Rome. Also, it would have to move quickly enough for the rapidly descending sun to have one last peep from beneath it. It was cat and mouse and hugely exciting. One widespread splash of hard sunlight to bathe the middle distance and the clump of cypress in light, while the dark and boiling cloak of rain cloud hung above, was what I craved. The ideal would be for the foreground to remain in partial shadow, encouraging the eye to be pulled onto the soft green baize where the dark green cypress trees stood.

I had a large piece of black plastic sheeting draped over both the tripod and me. No more than twenty minutes passed when the rain stopped and I was convinced I felt a rise in temperature on my back. I threw the sheet to one side and, in a flurry of excitement, prepared. It was if the entire scene had been choreographed, even to being presented with the shadow in the foreground, which I realized was produced by the road bridge behind me. In less than a minute the sun fell behind the last waiting cloud (there is almost always one) on the horizon behind me and, as is so often the case, the moment evaporated.

I have known this collection of trees for very many years and I know they are familiar to many a landscape photographer. The isolation of the trees in a sea of wine-bottle green turns the heads of probably two thousand car drivers a day, as these star performers are placed a few metres to the right of a fast double track road. It used to be dangerous to stop, and many a horn would blast as I jumped over the metal barricade. In 2003 the Italian road engineers took pity on photographers and constructed two parking places. Perhaps it was more to pre-empt accidents.

There are many photographers who have yet to discover Tuscany and these trees for the first time. I am sure they will not be disappointed. No doubt they too may experience a frisson as the light falls on these trees in the way that they would like. For me they offered their best performance on that wet day in May and I will ask nothing more of them.

# Balchladich Bay
## Scotland

Film **Fuji Velvia**
Camera **Hasselblad 6cmx6cm**
Lens **50mm**
Exposure **8 seconds f.22**
Filters **ND uniform 3 stop and ND graduated 1.5 stop and 81C**

This image was completely unexpected. I had gone to the north west of Ullapool with my nephew and, each with our cameras, we set off with a driven feeling of being on a mission. We could not have known that in the last twenty minutes of light, we would be offered such drama in both sea and sky.

Many landscape photographers gravitate to Scotland and I dare say we probably all share the same reasons for doing so: the feeling of being where man may never have trod, the wilderness areas like Rannoch Moor, the solitude, the contrast between this region and perhaps our own home environment, the quiet and the utter stillness of a sharp winter dawn where all is frozen and suspended, or the raging anger of a storm across the Cuillins where you feel that the landscape and sea may be scraped away from itself, with you and it lifted as one, up and away and whirled into the sky.

In the early or late hours, light intensity is low, but to correctly expose the image, which is of course paramount, the procedures are much the same as they would be at any other time of the day.

I had no expectations that the fat wedge of cloud might give some threat of rain at the top right hand corner, but I do remember the surface area being similar to the slabs of rock. The light was a low winter light and accordingly warm in nature – but was it warm enough? A filter can make a potentially good photograph better, but it cannot make an inherently bad photograph good. I chose to use the 81C, a uniform amber filter, and all that was warm became warmer, while the coolness was raised in colour temperature. I slightly regret the subtle milky green water losing some of its quality as a result.

After choosing an aperture, the shutter speed needs to be adjusted. Essentially, this equation must be adhered to, to ensure correct exposure. Using a uniform neutral density filter allowed me to break away from this mandatory configuration, thereby giving me more latitude.

But it is never just a technical exercise in these situations; this business is not about swooping into a remote location like a vulture, aiming and stealing a piece of landscape. The process is reciprocal, much more two-way than that; the whole thing is about engaging and about the ultimate enrichment from this exchange. The less there is of this, the less is the reward.

There was a good deal of noise on that cold and wet winter evening, but my reward was threefold wet, deafened and content.

# Rydal Water, Cumbria
## England

Film **Kodak Ektachrome 64asa**
Camera **Hasselblad 6cmx6cm**
Lens **50mm**
Exposure **1 second at f.22**
Filters **1sec. f.32**

Of all the lakes in Cumbria, Rydal Water is, I think, the lake that I love best. On a perfectly still morning the hills beyond and the surface of the water are fused by the wonderful phenomenon of reflection. Sunlight has no business here, for the entire scene is lit by light diffused by cloud. I had been standing on a small aluminium stepladder for about an hour or so since dawn, watching the ebb and flow of mist moving up and through the valley, sometimes surrounding me and then in a moment concealing the boat-shed altogether. Like a wandering phantom it seemed to be undecided, never settling for any moment. Then the lightest breeze lifted it away and up towards the distant hill, evaporating quickly and leaving me with Rydal Water revealed in the softest light. The stillness was palpable and in a moment a gentle watercolour emerged in front of my eyes.

From my vantage point nearly eight foot above the ground, the mildest of meanders is conveyed, with the Z-shape of water taking up a similar amount of surface area as the reeds. All could unfold towards me with every plane explained and with the distant neutral grey mountain providing the perfect unobtrusive backdrop.

It seems to me that many of those who photograph tend to do so from the height at which they stand, when a lower angle, often as little as a few centimetres, may radically alter the whole feel of the image. Equally, a higher vantage-point can reveal planes that might have become masked by others nearer to the camera. The great poverty of the photograph is, of course, its two dimensional nature: invest the image with depth, and the viewer is invited to walk in and onwards to the far distance.

I left this spot feeling as though I had departed from a secret place, back into the known world. The loud horn of a passing car facilitated the transition.

# Venice
## Italy

Film **Agfapan 25asa**
Camera **Hasselblad 6cmx6cm**
Lens **50mm**
Exposure **Not recorded**
Filters **Darkroom toning/bleaching**

It was a great privilege to have been asked to do my own book on Venice. I was given some very good advice before embarking on it. 'Arrive in Venice, wander through it without a camera; absorb it all before doing any photography.' I was reminded of a small boy rushing to play with a new toy without reading the instructions and knowing only half of what was possible.

For three days I wandered through this semi-ethereal, fantasy city, which seemed to me more like the scheme of an eccentric designer, who had dreamed up a thousand set pieces for staging a drama that has been playing for more than a thousand years.

There is an aesthetic uniformity to the entire city that I do not believe exists elsewhere in the world (except perhaps for Havana in Cuba), and into all of this I was dropped as if by parachute with my camera.

Since that first step from the vaporetto into the city, I, like many millions of others, have become entranced by Venice. But it remains one of the most difficult places in the world for me to make images. It seems inappropriate and impossible to make literal images of Venice when much of the city is romantic and illusory.

Within a day or two I had realized that the predominant shape throughout Venice was the arc. Four hundred and ten bridges, countless gondolas, the rims of the straw boaters and the church domes and, duplicated in reflection, the arc epitomized by the great double bend of the Grand Canal, all told me that this glorious city of Venice was about roundness.

I had seen this gondola tied up near the bridge a few times as I returned to my lodgings. It never seemed to be in quite the right place to establish an interlocking of shapes. The day before I was due to go home, to an equally extraordinary picture of green fields and Friesian cows, I saw that the rope attached to the prow was slightly longer than before, allowing the gondola to shift a little as passing traffic created disturbance in the canal. I committed, loaded black and white film into the film back, set up camera and tripod and waited. With an echoing bellow from the bargee, a barge laden with the brilliant colours of tomatoes and oranges came swerving round the corner and passed my gondola, pushing its nose to a position almost under the bridge with its passing. For one lovely luxurious minute I could wait until the elaborate and proud prow would quietly drift backwards and, at the given moment, when bridge and prow interlocked, I depressed the shutter.

A second later, the relationship had disintegrated and with a broad grin on my face, I packed up to leave for the strange spotty cows and vivid green fields of England. The whole thing had been really rather lovely.

# The See, Normandy
## France

I have a great fondness for this photograph. My father taught me to sail and from a young age I had come to understand something of boats.

It is obviously much more than about the boat being simply utilitarian. It must also surely be about grace, rhythm and just simply for me, anyway, as a nine year old, the fundamental pleasure of being on the water. Perhaps there is a nine year old to be found in many a sailor or in those who have an affection for steam trains.

A diagonal line drawn though Jersey and Guernsey brings you to a point just a few kilometres north of the bay of Mont St Michel, the great pilgrim destination. The See Estuary near Avranches, Normandy is slippery and shiny at low tide and I found it the perfect time to make this photograph. How convenient that the tide left this sleek boat suspended on a grassy tuft fulcrum, so perfectly balanced that I wondered if it had been laid to rest in this precise manner so that I could appreciate it. I felt sure it had.

The lit nearside gunwhale, the single seat and the two rowlocks attracted me as much as the hull. It was a thing of such beauty just settled there. I could appreciate the hull in a way that one normally cannot. The best bit is always hidden under water.

I can sometimes hear an elderly chum of mine declaring to me that if I were to pursue landscape photography then I must always remember that old piece of advice 'foreground interest' and here with my boat, I was supplying foreground interest smack-bang centre stage.I would not have wished to move the hull one inch, but I do remember stretching as high as I possibly could so that a strip of muddy foreshore was revealed on the other side. I hoped that I could hold some detail in the nearside hull as the dark green grass was unlikely to reflect back any light toward it and essentially the entire scene was backlit.

When I first began landscape photography, I enjoyed studying the Zone system through the Ansel Adams books. 'Expose for the shadows and develop for the highlights,' was my favourite adage. It took me months to grasp, but Ansel Adams and his brilliant artistic/scientific approach to his work, along with his rigorous darkroom discipline I have not seen matched and probably never will.

Finally, the sky performed wonderfully on cue. Some fairly shallow cumulus, sweeping in across Mont St Michel and beyond from the Atlantic, delivered themselves to me like a gift, their puffy edges leaving white freckled reflections.

I care for the small chain hanging vertically from the bow, reminding this lovely craft of its owner and its obligations. All she had to do for me however was rest, just where she had been randomly laid by the tide.

Film **Kodak Technical Pan**
Camera **Hasselblad 6cmx6cm**
Lens **50mm**
Exposure **1 sec f.22**
Filters **Orange filter**

# Rovereto
## Italy

Film **Fuji 50asa**
Camera **Hasselblad 6cmx6cm**
Lens **250mm**
Exposure **1 sec f.32**
Filters **Polarizer**

It is no secret that I have a passion for investing a landscape photograph with as much depth as possible, when possible. The great poverty of painting, photography and film is its two-dimensional nature and with my photography I am always trying to mitigate this. Movies filmed to enable the viewer to see everything in three dimensions with the aid of special glasses, would find me in the front row staring up with astonishment at the depth of every scene. The desire to reach out and touch everything is irresistible. Despite the wonderful technological advances we have made, I am amazed that all films these days are not produced in 3-D.

On my way north to Trento and bound for a pass into Switzerland, I left the main road and drove slightly west and north again, choosing what I hoped would be a more interesting road for photography. For five weeks I had been away from England working on a book on many regions of Italy and had become creatively exhausted. It was time to go home.

I was not sure whether there had been a marble quarry here but it certainly did not look as if this layered strata was a natural phenomenon.

I had looked at this extraordinary building for some time before making the decision to set up the camera. It was raining and I thought that there was insufficient light to provide some modelling that would give relief to the house. I was unsure whether the rock and house could fit into a square format with the two triangles of rock and vegetation using up the top right and bottom left of the square. I felt that the continuity was broken and that the photograph would be more powerful if the entire image comprised the house and blue rock and nothing else. I tried very hard to make that possible but the house was positioned too near to the lower diagonal division of rock and vegetation.

These long wedges of rock, stacked up perfectly like an immaculately layered trifle, were too good to pass by and their vivid blue colouring was unlike anything I had ever seen before. I had seen blue sodalite rock in Namibia but never anything this blue in Italy.

I am very fond of a polarizing filter in low light, as there is always some white light reflection to be removed from one plane or another, especially on upper surfaces reflecting the sky. Using it here helped saturate the blues and emphasize the apparent blue vertical staining.

But who lived here? The house with its fitting patina of pink, blue and white could not have been occupied. I was as much involved with its story as with the photograph and it was only when I turned to collect my belongings that I thought I saw a figure in the arched doorway to the left. But of course I could not have.

# Val d'Orcia, Tuscany

## Italy

Twenty-two years ago, while working in Italy, I chose to turn east from the Via Cassia towards Rome, and took a road no doubt familiar to many a local Tuscan, but not to me. I could never have known that over the next twenty years or so, I would be travelling by foot and car along both this road and every back road in the region perhaps more than a hundred times. This thirty kilometre stretch and the *strada biancas* that radiate to the north and south of it remains the loveliest areas of all Italy for me. Like an old misshapen lumpy mattress, this chalk and clay landscape is classic Tuscany. My recollection then was of dilapidated farmhouses crowning every bump, complete with a cluster of guardian cypress trees.

Now in the twenty-first century, the ramshackle farmhouses have been transformed into large mansions with perfect avenues of immature cypress leading

Film **Fuji Velvia**
Camera **Fuji 6cm x 17cm**
Lens **300mm**
Exposure **8 seconds f.64**
Filters **Polarizer and ND 1 stop graduated**

up to perfect thresholds. Cranes on the brows of hills betray restoration of the few old houses that remain.

A piece of my heart belongs to this ravishing landscape. To be up at 5am on a May dawn, especially after a night's rainfall, looking down and across the Val d'Orcia is utterly beautiful.

When this image was made, there was a moment some half hour before sun up when the mist seemed to be like swirling chiffon, sometimes so dense that I was smothered. Within a moment or two it would become diaphanous, diffusing the early light. A 6cm x 17cm panoramic camera seemed fitting to use here. I deliberately chose to drop the hilltop into the middle of the image and the vast breadth of the panoramic camera allowed all the agreeable shapes and the recession of the distant hills to fall into place.

Looking at this image now, I sometimes wonder whether it was a fairy-tale setting and that I just happened to be there to see it manifest into reality… for a moment or two.

# The Dordogne
## France

Film **Kodak 64asa**
Camera **Hasselblad 6cmx6cm**
Lens **80mm**
Exposure ½ **f.32**

I have thoroughly enjoyed this image for many years. But, having said that, it is important that with this particular one, I should admit to a failure of perception both pre- and post-natal.

The very instant that a potential image formulates in my mind continues to preoccupy me. I am happy to admit that a good few avenues of trees are to be seen among the pages of this book. There was a time when I felt that this was merely a retreat to known territory, like the composer who, battling with inspiration and momentarily at sea, is tempted back into a melody that has been tried and proven. However, gardeners, cooks and all creative folk have a style they feel disinclined to depart from. Photographers are no different. I am happy to remain with a stately avenue of trees to provide me with the order that I seek.

Some years ago I was giving a talk to a group of photographers and when this image appeared, a retired brigadier in the British army bellowed out from the back of the auditorium: 'What a damn fine bottle of Chardonnay!' I looked as if for the first time and with an exclamation of amazement I saw the perfectly proportioned shape of a wine bottle in the middle. I was horrified that I had failed to see it when I had made the image all those years ago and with some embarrassment congratulated the Brigadier on his powers of observation – not for a moment revealing that I had never noticed. Now of course it is quite impossible for me to look at this image without seeing the bottle of Chardonnay.

As with the image on page 53 there is a certain secrecy to this Dordogne avenue. I enjoy the brightness emerging through each tree with the brightly lit maze lying along the base and the sliver of sunlight beneath. One of the pleasures of working in a stand of poplar trees is the nature of the trees' bark. Had the bark been darker, then the image would probably not have been possible, as the trees would have been seen in silhouette – a style I have never cared for. Detail, when possible, is the key; thankfully, the tonal value of the bark was sufficient to allow the viewer to see its nature. At the end, I chose to walk through this elegant line of trees, and the experience was rather like wandering backstage at a theatre. I had been observing the performance for some time and to walk amongst the cast was strangely enjoyable.

# Chesil Beach, Dorset
## England

Film **Fuji Velvia**
Camera **Hasselblad 6cmx6cm**
Lens **50mm**
Exposure **1/15th sec f.11**
Filters **ND 1.5 stop graduated**

Chesil Beach is near my home in the south of England and on a calm day, in still air, it might be thought that nothing much ever happens here; just the usual repetitive lapping of the waves against the pebbly shore.

Yet once it may have done and in a grand and cataclysmic fashion. Some people believe that a giant wave crashed over the bank of pebbles, pouring the ocean with one heave into the lowland behind. There are several records, some very early, of violent seas surging and driving over the Chesil bank with fishermen's houses, villages and lives lost. As I write, the world weeps for Asia and her lost lives.

After the violence, the sea once again becomes calm, admitting nothing, innocent of any charge. But I have stood at this spot many times, mesmerized by the two rectangular solids of water and sky, and remembering the voices of mariner friends whispering of the sea, 'Never underestimate her.'

When I planned this trip, the local forecast had been correct, except for precisely when the cloud would begin to break. It was not until half an hour before sunset that the hitherto solid cloud seemed to fracture and open in lightning-like zig-zags, allowing sunlight to slice through.

I used a simple yet crucial neutral density graduated filter here. Happily the brightness range between sky and sea was not too great, thanks to the predominance of heavy dark cloud; a one and a half stop filter was all that was necessary. There are times when I like to emphasize the warmth that prevails at the time and I chose to do so by introducing an 81C amber filter.

Over the years I have been astonished by the colours of some skies and am often unable to believe that they are real. I have observed the light at sunset with accompanying clouds often reflecting the long rays of yellow, orange and red, conveying colours so extreme to my eye that I would only have expected to see them on a canvas by Turner. There is a peak to these divine moments which is always held for a moment or two, suspended for us to savour and admire. Then the sky is drained of colour as grey takes hold and we stand there as if it was all an illusion.

But why should we not see every colour in the visible spectrum in the sky? I think I may have seen almost all colours imaginable, even green fringes to great continents of cumulonimbus cloud bulging with rain.

On this day, there was an explosive feel in the sky as if there might be some unexpected event. The sea fell onto the billion pebbles of Chesil Beach in much the same way it always has. But I remember perversely imagining that the horizon was consuming the sun, biting into it in a series of smooth arcs, until finally there was just a slim red finger nail remaining and then dusk was in attendance.

# Mont Sainte Victoire

## France

I have always had a fixation with small sheds. I am not ashamed of this – there must be a psychological reason for such fondness for Lilliputian dwellings.

Staying in the handsome city of Aix-en-Provence in southern France, I was lamenting my delay in arriving. The summer had been dry and autumn was uncharacteristically early; the viticulturist whose land lay along the lower slopes of Mont Sainte Victoire had long since harvested his crop, and the vines, with just a few ragged leaves, were stripped of grapes. But I had seen a shed!

The first moment of recognition that there is an image to be made continues to fascinate me. Perhaps the response is stimulated by an instant appreciation of some apparent aesthetic cohesion; a whistle-stop tour of all the 'bits' that make up the whole. At worst the impulse is driven by a formulaic library of 'what works'. These sit like dependable long-term investments in my memory bank of past images made and past influential images seen, variations being called upon when stimulated by matched and recognizable components in a landscape. Whichever activation key lies behind the compulsion to make an image (I like to think it is not the library but fresh eyes greeting new opportunities), the joy of discovery is beyond description.

The recognition of an image 'in waiting' seems to occur in a millisecond and what appears to be a sublimely perfect image is formulated in my mind without fault or aberration. It is then that I work with the mechanics to produce an image that will come as near as possible to the one I can picture. It is asking what lies in front of me to comply with what resides in my imagination.

My humble little shed (and it was mine for that time) arrived like falling in love. The dusting of orange light on its chunky stone work was a gift, as was its dark doorway which provided the point of deep black which, to a certain extent, images need somewhere – although not taking up too much of the surface area. Deep black nothingness gives little to the viewer.

There was a delightful though perhaps tenuous relationship between the mountain, the tiled roof of my shed and the rumpled soil. The deep corrugated clefts in Mont Sainte Victoire were not quite dense enough in their shadows, but with the pale limestone ridges reflecting each into its neighbouring hollow, they acted well as a rudimentary 'fill in'. The final player in the scene was the cirrocumulus sky, each puff much more entertaining than a carpet of infinite blue.

Twenty years later, I returned, hoping to find my shed. The search was in vain but I was reminded of the changes that would have taken place since Cezanne sat with his easel below these slopes, as he painted this long whale of a mountain some eighty or so times. Perhaps the shed belonged not to me, but to Cezanne.

Film **Kodak Ektachrome**
Camera **Hasselblad 6cmx6cm**
Lens **50mm**
Exposure **½ f.22**
Filters **Polarizer**

Mont Sainte Victoire, France 

# Near Stonehenge, Wiltshire
## England

Film **Kodak Ektachrome 64asa**
Camera **Hasselblad 6cmx6cm**
Lens **50mm**
Exposure **½ sec f.22**
Filters **Polarizer**

As a boy I remember traipsing behind the baler in late August, and with a sense of monumental achievement, heaving rectangular bales up onto the trailer, fingers raw with cuts from the coarse binder twine. In the late seventies the familiar brick-shaped bale was soon to be eclipsed by the much more glamorous cylinder. Here was true and natural glowing installation-art sitting on the stubble.

When I came across these five-foot high bales, I was disappointed. The sky was weak: a dreary monotonous blue with no information, no fun. But from the angle at which I stood, I thought the farmer must have seen me coming. There before me was a series of bales that were positioned like a perfectly laid table. Of the eleven Swiss-roll bales, two sets seemed inseparable from one another. There was only one position from which to make this image – often the case. The more certain I am that the place where the tripod legs dig into the ground is the one and only place, the greater my confidence that the image will succeed. I looked across to the west and saw a formation of cloud that made me laugh out loud. It was beyond belief that such an arrangement of building cumulus cloud could echo so precisely the giant bales beneath. But the clouds were some kilometres away and by the time the boiling masses arrived, they would no longer mirror so well the shape of the bales.

The nature of young, fair-weather, building cumuli is one of expansion and likely subsequent disintegration; but, palms together, I pleaded with them to be delivered with the prevailing wind and to position themselves perfectly above my bales. I could not keep my eyes from the sky and, as every moment passed, I wondered if the design would collapse. The far clouds became more slender with the leading cloud still in place, as they slowly progressed towards their predestined position. This was pure theatre, and, as at Lake Titicaca (page 44), I felt that other forces were at work here.

Then, as if with a trumpet voluntary, the entire ensemble came together and it all seemed perfect. But it was not. I could see through the viewfinder of my camera the telltale shadow of my tripod. I had no choice. Had I moved two inches down on the tripod, the base of the leading cloud would have been intercepted by the top of the large bale in the foreground. Two inches to my left and the division between the foreground bale and the bale to its right would have been interrupted. An inch or so to my right and the bale almost on the horizon to the left would have been concealed. I was stuck. Surely there was a compromise to be found? Yet compromise is the most unwelcome word in any artistic endeavour. I wanted to make my image of the bales on this glorious day in Wiltshire from exactly this point in the field and from nowhere else. It may seem sentimental but as I left this place, I said thank you.

# Skye
## Scotand

Film **Fuji 100asa**
Camera **Hasselblad 6cmx6cm**
Lens **50mm**
Exposure **$\frac{1}{8}$th f.22**
Filters **ND 1 stop graduated**

For a landscape photographer, an opportunity to journey and photograph in the highlands and glens of Scotland is impossible to resist, especially in winter. Why should this be so? Why would many a landscape photographer prefer to photograph in this land than the soft lowlands of perhaps the Sussex downs? Both regions have a quality; the Sussex downs are particularly lovely in early summer. The rolling fields are covered in a snowfall of oxeye daisies, and the great chalky Seven Sisters cliffs near Eastbourne glow under their mantle of fresh green.

I have great fondness for the gentle topography of the south, as with the image of The Manger in Berkshire on page 58, but this is no 'butch' landscape. Its wildernesses have long since been harnessed for human use. So, for a more primitive, hard-edged landscape, I will readily turn to the Scottish Highlands, untamed and unchanged.

Take this rock: nothing unusual about it, but if you were to lift it from its natural context, where it would not have been given a second glance, and drop it into a meadow near Brighton, southerners would be bewildered. Some installation art form or a contemporary sculpture perhaps?

I marched across a peaty unpredictable Skye landscape to be near this fine rock and to understand its relationship with the serrated mountain outline beyond. I felt that this lump had a certain importance; it would have been here for an eternity. Why would anyone want to have moved it? With the aid of a small stepladder I was able to gain a little elevation, allowing me to lay the apex of the rock into the mountain hollow on the skyline. I have rarely stretched so high to tuck a top under a distant skyline and although the tiptoe stretch for the image made in Bolivia at Titicaca (page 44) is hard to beat, this was rather more difficult because of the spongy ground underfoot. A stepladder is precarious enough when reaching to paint a high ceiling but hoping for stability in a peat bog on the island of Skye in a damp November was something akin to tightrope walking.

I made a few images of this rock with the sky in different states of menace and, looking now at the breach in the rain cloud, I have a sense of the rock ripping through the cloud cover and plunging like a meteoric fireball down to earth.

Of course, I am quite happy to admit that there is something of a little post-rationalization coming into play here, as I patently did not imagine this romantic notion at the time of making the image – I was too cold.

Yet, I was truly aware of the sky and the pathos of the moment; the romantic aspect of the story is an afterthought, but why not?

# Wadi Rum
## Jordan

Standing alone in Wadi Rum in the bright yet half-light of dawn is definitely to be recommended to anyone who loves the movie *Lawrence of Arabia*. I was here with my great friend Richard, who has seen it many times and knows it well. It was his idea that we should travel to this remarkable desert in Jordan.

The imagined voices of David Lean and Freddie Young, the great cinematographer, plus hundreds of crew, cast and caterers, were more than palpable that morning as we waited for the sun to rise. (I remember reading that in the crew there had been two noble property men, brothers I believe, who earned themselves a reputation for sweeping the desert clean of footprints and tyre tracks.)

It was said of Lean that he wanted his movies to comprise a series of still images, each one perfectly designed, shaped and refined and all brought together to make a moving whole. My friend Richard knew all there was to know about the film and its making and I was grateful to him for bringing it alive for me that day.

I have always been enthusiastic about continuing to make black and white images despite some people's surprise at my doing so. The absence of colour can often distil the image down to its essential qualities, which I enjoy attempting to reveal. Despite the medium of black and white being an abstraction, and so far away from colour, which I work with predominantly, I very much enjoy it.

As the light rose over the humps in the desert and temperature changes evolved, I could see the sky was gathering an identity that would be soon be offered to me. With a red filter I felt the burst of cloud racing across the sky from some unknown point to the right would be more pronounced in black and white.

I knew the camel and his owner would be there, and to this day I am glad that I did not shout in my best Arabic to ask him to pause. It is important that the camel's front and rear left legs convey movement and that his big jaw is open and his tail swishes. I made a few exposures as the camel and his rider moved towards the centre of the frame. At that point, despite countless voices echoing in my ears about not placing the focal point in the heart of the image, I felt compelled to do so. The black stripe of shadow, cast by a pinnacle of rock to the east, provided the perfect road along which the two could travel. Two more strides from the camel and its owner's head would have been sliced off by the brightly lit slope beyond. That would have been so catastrophic as to have rendered the image useless. David Lean would never have tolerated such a thing.

Film **Konica Infrared**
Camera **Hasselblad 6cmx6cm**
Lens **80mm**
Exposure **1/8 sec f.16**
Filters **25A red filter**

Wadi Rum, Jordan 

# Erme Mouth, Devon
## England

Film **Kodak Ektachrome 64**
Camera **Hasselblad 6cmx6cm**
Lens **50mm**
Exposure **¼ f.22**
Filters **Polarizer**

This was one of the earliest landscape photographs I made and, despite having lived with it for many years, I still care for it very much.

It is not an image with dramatic light; in fact the light source was diffused and the sky not ideal. I prefer a sky with a little more bite to it and more definition, but this sky was right for these rocks.

I had been working in Devon for a while and decided to visit an estuary I had never seen before. The River Erme is not well known, nor does it have the reputation of being one of the country's great five-star estuaries, but on that day it proved well worth the journey from Dartmouth where I had been staying.

I walked along the edge of the estuary, watching the tide bringing in new water. It came in with tremendous speed, forcing me up the beach to the shoreline to keep my feet dry. After a few hundred metres with nothing alerting me enough to make an investment, I turned to go back while there was still time. In a moment this image became clear to me; I suppose I would have seen it earlier, had I glanced back, as I often do, on the off chance.

As I set up, with nobody nearby, I cursed the previous walker who had left large and very conspicuous footprints in the sand. I stooped down to begin the task of removing them, with a bunch of seaweed for a broom. I realized of course that the culprit was me; my very recognizable feet were to blame.

There is a feeling here that the entire collection of rocks is made of some synthetic material and that at any moment an opera singer will emerge and launch into a great aria. The scene looks only half real: every time I look at it, I become intrigued as to why this should be so. Of course, the dark sky above contributes, by not stealing the eye away from the interest; there is no vast, sharply defined, building cumulus to compete with, which would have been inappropriate. The pale green field and the ice blue strip of water play their parts too.

I am not alone in my response to this image as being slightly odd; friends have observed the same. If I had had my stepladder with me, I would have raised myself by a foot or so to allow the rock to the left to tuck beneath the green hill beyond. This would have improved the image by revealing the continuity of the entire field.

I know that I could probably remove the marks of my footsteps in the sand using digital software but, in fact, I would much rather go back to that beach, and that time in my life, and do it myself.

# Pamplona
## Spain

Film **Kodak Ektachrome**
Camera **Hasselblad 6cmx6cm**
Lens **150mm**
Exposure **½ sec f.22**
Filters **Polarizer and ND 1 stop graduated**

There are many images I have seen over the years that elicit the response: 'That looks so surreal'. This one of Pamplona often draws the same comment. The surrealist movement is broadly thought of as 'dreamlike', 'an expression of the subconscious mind', the 'irrational juxtaposition of images', a feeling of not being 'real'. Perhaps real is also the known. Numerous photographers were engaging with this popular style, predominantly in black and white, and many images made during the period are now highly collectable and of great value.

I had been staying in Pamplona some one hundred and fifty kilometres due south of Biarritz, for a day or two, and had investigated this reservoir to the east three times. A man-made reservoir rarely has the character of a natural lake. After all, there was never meant to be water in a valley where villages have been drowned in order to satisfy the vast urban demand for it. Reservoirs carry with them these negative connotations and, even if there are no emotional associations for me, I am rarely drawn to these apparently unauthentic bodies of water. But this reservoir, known as Embalse de Yesa, had a quality on the fourth visit that I had not detected before. Here was certainly a feeling of the surreal; of a landscape with a look that was completely unfamiliar to me – a look of the illusory.

In almost every case, trees are greater in height than humans and as we go about our daily lives we expect generally to be overshadowed by the taller tree. How peculiar it felt to be looking down on these cypress trees, a few of which had their tips piercing the water surface. But why surreal? Could it be the still pure silence of the scene? More than that surely. Is it something to do with the sky, which seems to rush from the horizon towards the spectator, enfolding us in a soft blue/grey cloak? The two hills either side, with their mild gradient leading the eye towards the centre of the image clearly must play some part.

With expansive views, the two-dimensional nature of photography is most difficult to mitigate, and is often achieved by the distribution of light-revealing planes, which provide the precious element of depth. Yet there appears to be a depth that already sweeps the onlooker into, through and onwards to the end of the image.

I do take issue with this image, however. Among the unpleasant features of a reservoir are its edges. Here the unlawful water laps uncomfortably at a once gently sloping meadow, where an armada of bulldozers have torn away at the landscape in preparation for the flood. The edges of the image to the right are most unsatisfactory to me, disfigured and harsh. But, safe above the flood, the small village with its church at the centre remains, a sturdy reminder of stability and hope. Perhaps the essence of this image is its holiness.

# Sossusvlei

## Namibia

We set off well before dawn. The stars were bright, and the prospect of another drive down the sixty deeply potholed kilometres to the dunes was, as always, very exciting. I have made this journey several times and I always feel heroic as we thunder down the track. Meanwhile, I can't help looking upwards to see what the sky is doing. I noticed that the once brilliant stars were now becoming less so. This could mean only one thing: cloud. It was already clear that there would be no decent light at all. But a photographer friend used to say: 'Just a little further along the road'. With that in mind, we pushed on.

Film **Agfapan 25as**
Camera **Hasselblad Xpan**
Lens **90mm**
Exposure **2 sec f.22**
Filters **Orange filter**

Having been here not twelve hours before for the evening light, I knew where I would set up my tripod and the panoramic camera. I was not hopeful. I reckoned that in less than twenty minutes, there would be total cloud cover and the dunes would become a shapeless mass of bland sand. Incredibly, the sun burnt its way through and blasted the dunes with hard light, leaving the sky looking like diffused sequins. I was ready to work in black and white with some very slow Agfapan 25 high contrast film.

I have always loved that zone between the lit and the unlit. In the far dunes where there are sharp 45 degree angles, the separation of lit and unlit is blade-sharp. In the foreground the gradual nature of a dune at much less of an angle, gives way to shadow as the light runs out. The wind patterns in the sand look with low oblique light like snake skin. This image shows the dunes staggering rhythm and geometry.

# Old Leigh, Essex
## England

Film **Fujichrome 50 asa**
Camera **Hasselblad**
Lens **150mm**
Exposure **1 sec f.22**
Filters **ND graduated .45**

It has always been hard to turn away from any possibility of making images of water. I know of no landscape photographers who do not care for water.

I had been encouraged to come here for a dawn photograph and after a fair forecast, there seemed to be a good chance. Dawn is always tantalizing: the nature of light that one has wished for may never materialize yet another unlooked for image may emerge in front of one's eyes. That is one of the most wonderful things about landscape photography that is rarely discussed: the element of surprise can be as joyful as it can be in photojournalism.

The river Thames has its focal point in the city of London where it is flanked by some of the finest architecture of the land. To Londoners the Thames is 'their' river. The Londoner who can see with ease the entire breadth of the river takes ownership of just that segment flowing past their window. In the heart of the city, the twisting nature of the curvature of the river offers people living on different axes entirely different mornings and evenings to those enjoyed at the river's mouth.

Further east, following the Thames on its northern shore, the people of Old Leigh have yet another relationship with the river. Here this mighty waterway seems to have broken away from its urban snaking confines and, with its breadth, belongs to all. No longer does she vacillate restlessly from corner to corner: from these northern shores the folk here can look south across some miles of estuary. Throughout the year their gaze may often be accompanied with a comment to their neighbour as to 'the look of her today'.

Photographing here where, at its ebb and flow, the river expresses itself so beautifully, I am able to see the land beneath momentarily revealed: great shallow hollows of backlit burnished brass at sunset or, after a cool sunrise, calm oval pools stretched out collecting blue light from the broken sky above and reflecting back to my camera. The water's edge is a lovely place to be at the first and last of the day.

I rarely hear of people leaving a water-side home. To part company and move inland must bring a remorse and sense of loss for all the dependable passive company the water gave. Like friendship with a tree, there can be a silent dialogue with water, with its constant unrepeating motion and its soft echo of the sky above. For a landscape photographer, that exchange can be both profound and intense.